KS2 English Comprehension

Teacher Book 2 — Years 3-6

This Teacher book accompanies CGP's **second set** of Targeted Comprehension Question Books for Years 3-6.

It includes helpful introductions to every text, answers to each question, ideas for extension activities, pupil progress charts… and more.

All in all, everything you need to plan and organise your Guided Reading sessions throughout KS2!

Contents

Key Stage Two Reading Comprehension 1
The Targeted Question Books 2
The Teacher Book 3
Planning and Delivery 4
Marking and Monitoring Progress 5
Genre Charts 6
Cross-Curricular Subject Charts 10

Year 3

The Three Nanny Goats Gruff by Louise McEvoy 14
An Interview with Andy Seed from www.booktrust.org.uk 15
Pioneer Children by Brenda Williams 16
The Reluctant Dragon by Kenneth Grahame 17
Poems about Teachers by Peter Dixon and Kenn Nesbitt 18
Caring for Dogs and Puppies by Ben Hubbard 19
Mr Gum and the Biscuit Billionaire by Andy Stanton 20
Echo Effects by John Clark 21
Chicken School by Jeremy Strong 22
Plastic Bag Tree by Michael Rosen 23
Sky Island by L. Frank Baum 24
Labels on Children's Food from The Independent 25
Oliver Twist by Charles Dickens 26
Nepal Earthquake Appeal from www.savethechildren.org.uk 27
Sir Gawain and the Green Knight by Michael Morpurgo 28

Year 4

The Diary of a Killer Cat by Anne Fine 29
Geocaching from The Telegraph 30
The Dragonsitter's Island by Josh Lacey 31
GRRRR by Francesca Beard 32

Julius Caesar's Goat by Dick King-Smith 33
Armoured Dinosaurs by Louise McEvoy 34
The Story of Nu Wa by Holly Robinson 35
Coram Boy by Helen Edmundson 36
An Interview with Tim Peake from www.destinationspace.uk 37
Escape from Germany by Penny McKinlay 38
Poems about the Weather by Robert Louis Stevenson and Carol Ann Duffy 39
Wayne Rooney: Captain of England by Tom and Matt Oldfield 40
The Lion, the Witch and the Wardrobe by C.S. Lewis 41
A Letter from Barack Obama 42
The Jungle Book by Rudyard Kipling 43

Year 5

Gertrude Ederle by Louise McEvoy 44
The Unluckiest Boy in the World by Andrew Norriss 45
Baby Birds from www.rspb.org.uk 46
Johnny and the Dead by Terry Pratchett and Stephen Briggs 47
Goodnight Mister Tom by Michelle Magorian 48
Facts about Hurricanes! from www.ngkids.co.uk 49
Poems about Words by Adisa and Maya Angelou 50
The Oak and the Linden Tree by Ovid 51
Cora and the King by Louise McEvoy 52
Robot on the Ice by Kimberly Shillcutt Tyree 53
Candara's Gift by Jasper Cooper 54
The Hound of the Baskervilles by Arthur Conan Doyle 55
Harambe the Gorilla from The Independent 56
The Highwayman by Alfred Noyes 57
Steve Jobs' Biography by Karen Blumenthal 58

Year 6

Talking Turkeys!! by Benjamin Zephaniah 59
Pig Heart Boy by Malorie Blackman 60
The Story of My Life by Helen Keller 61
The Lost Diary of Snow White by Boyd Brent 62
The Yellow Train from The Telegraph 63
David Copperfield by Charles Dickens 64
Edible Cutlery from www.dogonews.com 65
The Curse of the Gloamglozer by Paul Stewart and Chris Riddell 66
Malala Yousafzai from www.biographyonline.net 67
Poems about World War One by John McCrae and Moina Michael 68
Moonfleet by J. Meade Falkner 69
Beowulf the Warrior by Ian Serraillier 70
Cyber-Bullying from The Daily Mail 71
Romeo and Juliet by William Shakespeare 72
A Letter from a Former Slave by Jourdon Anderson 73

Pupil Progress Charts 74

When using the Extra Activities in this product, please take the safety of the participants into consideration at all times, and ensure that children are supervised when researching material for this product online. Teachers should also take into account pupils' personal circumstances when dealing with topics of a sensitive nature.

Published by CGP

Editors: Alex Fairer, Catherine Heygate, Louise McEvoy, Holly Robinson
Consultants: Maxine Petrie
Proofreaders: Samantha Bensted, Janet Berkeley, Amanda MacNaughton, Glenn Rogers, Karen Wells

With thanks to Ana Pungartnik for the copyright research.

ISBN: 978 1 78294 703 5
Printed by Elanders Ltd, Newcastle upon Tyne.
Illustrations on pages 14, 16, 19, 21, 26, 28, 29, 30, 34, 35, 36, 38, 44, 46, 47, 51, 54, 55, 62, 68, 69, 72 © clipart.com

Key Stage Two Reading Comprehension

In this introduction, you'll find everything you need to help you get the most out of CGP's second set of Key Stage Two Targeted Comprehension books.

Reading comprehension is a key part of the National Curriculum

The English Programme of Study for the Key Stage Two National Curriculum requires pupils to explore a wide variety of fiction and non-fiction texts. Pupils are expected to:

- develop increasingly advanced reading comprehension skills;
- expand their vocabulary;
- improve the accuracy and fluency with which they read;
- develop their ability to understand and make inferences about complex and challenging texts.

CGP's Key Stage Two Targeted Comprehension: Set Two

- CGP's Key Stage Two Targeted Comprehension range is designed to support the development and assessment of pupils' reading comprehension skills throughout years 3 to 6. It is ideal for use in Guided Reading sessions.
- The range is packed full of high-quality texts, from a variety of authors and sources, that will instil in pupils a love of reading and encourage them to read more widely and deeply.
- Set Two consists of four Targeted Question Books (see page 2 for more information)...

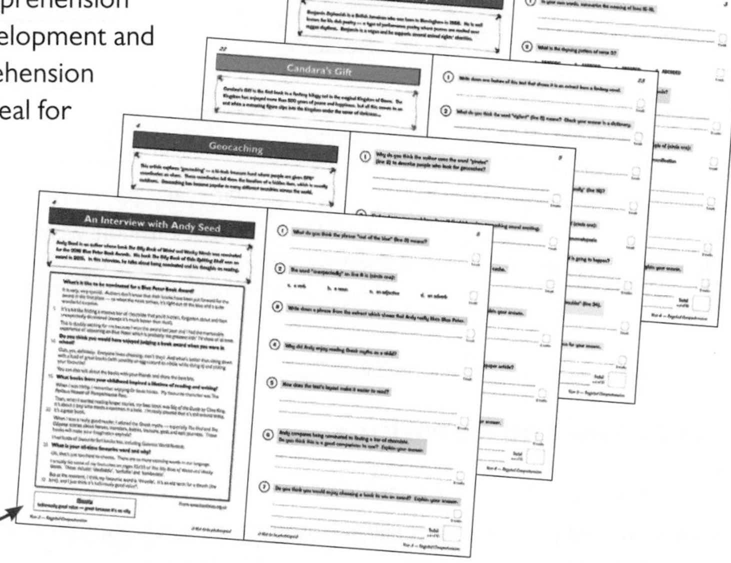

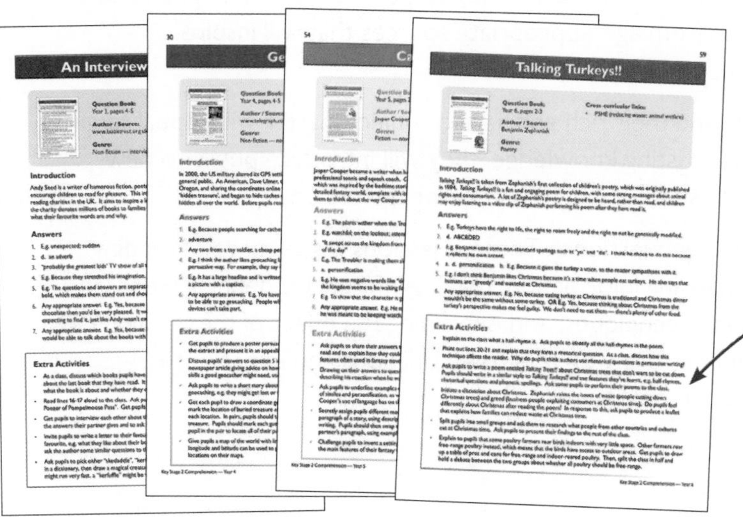

- ...and an accompanying Teacher Book. The range can be used in Guided Reading sessions, or as the foundation for a variety of other literacy lessons and activities.
- Many of the Extra Activities in the Teacher Book have been designed to support teaching across the whole Key Stage Two curriculum — see pages 3 and 4 for how to incorporate the texts into your scheme of work.

The Targeted Question Books

What are the Targeted Question Books?

The Key Stage Two Targeted Comprehension: Set Two includes four Targeted Question Books — one each for years 3, 4, 5 and 6. Each book contains fifteen engaging texts, accompanied by challenging and stimulating questions.

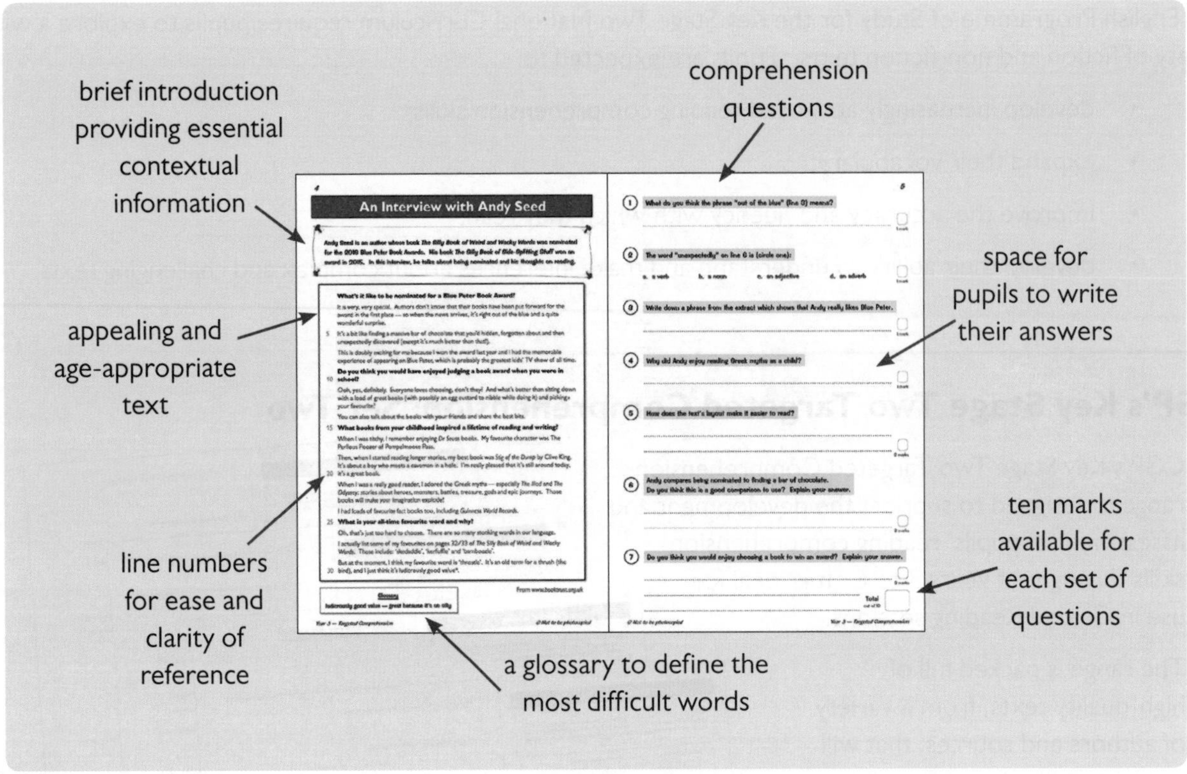

The texts and the questions

- Each Targeted Question Book includes a variety of fiction and non-fiction texts, drawn from different genres, including poetry, plays, classic and modern fiction, myths and legends, news articles, reference texts, diary entries, letters and autobiographical writing.
- The texts have been carefully chosen to capture the interest of Key Stage Two pupils and promote enjoyment of reading. They have been taken from age-appropriate sources that will inspire many pupils to read the rest of the text independently.
- The texts deal with a wide variety of topics, and their rich and varied subject matter will appeal to girls and boys alike. As well as building on pupils' existing knowledge, they will introduce pupils to new concepts and ideas that will often form the basis for thought-provoking discussions.
- Each text is followed by a set of comprehension questions. These questions test a range of reading comprehension skills: retrieving facts; summarising information; making inferences; defining words in context; identifying literary and presentational techniques; and explaining the effect of these techniques on the reader. Some questions require pupils to draw on their own opinions and experiences, encouraging them to relate to the text on a personal level.

The Teacher Book

What is the Teacher Book?

This Teacher Book will help you to use the texts in the Targeted Question Book Twos to their full potential, incorporating texts from all four books into your planning. It provides an introduction to each text, full answers to the questions in the Targeted Question Book Twos and suggestions for literacy-based and cross-curricular Extra Activities. Used together, the questions and Extra Activities will help pupils engage with and show they have understood the texts, as well as enabling you to assess and monitor the development of their comprehension skills.

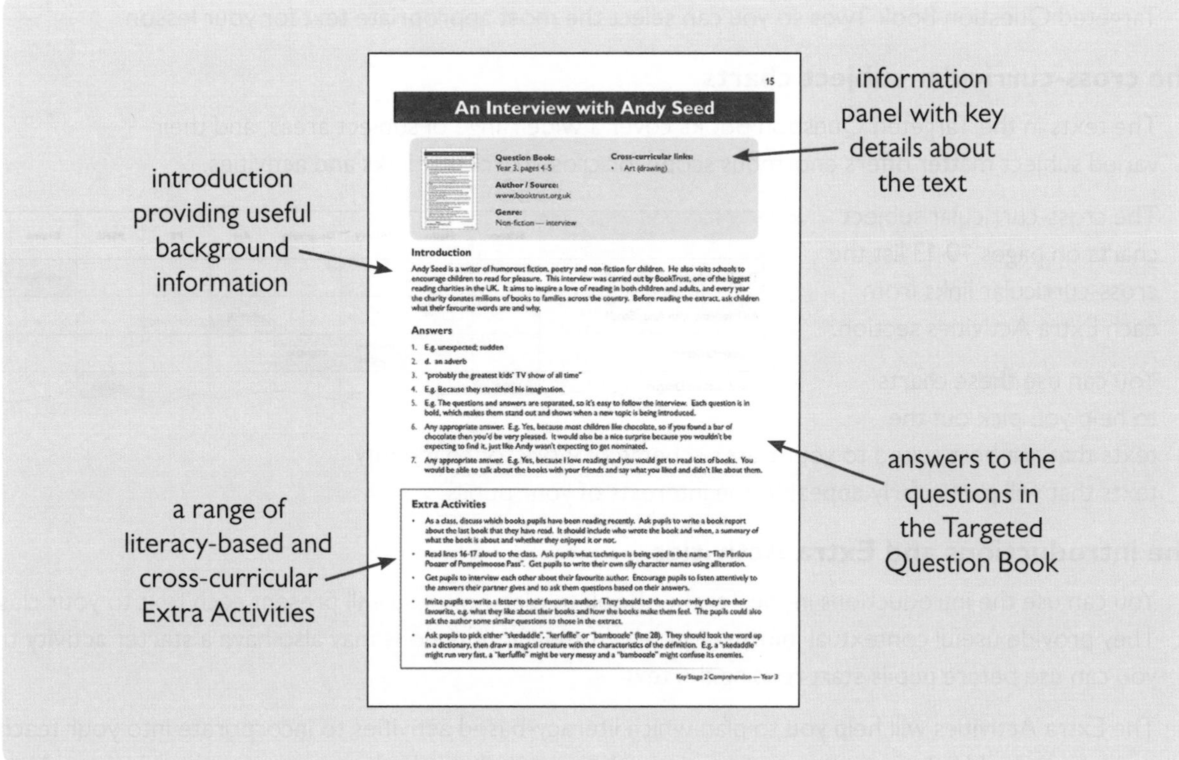

15

An Interview with Andy Seed

Question Book: Year 3, pages 4-5

Author / Source: www.booktrust.org.uk

Genre: Non-fiction — interview

Cross-curricular links:
- Art (drawing)

Introduction

Andy Seed is a writer of humorous fiction, poetry and non-fiction for children. He also visits schools to encourage children to read for pleasure. This interview was carried out by BookTrust, one of the biggest reading charities in the UK. It aims to inspire a love of reading in both children and adults, and every year the charity donates millions of books to families across the country. Before reading the extract, ask children what their favourite words are and why.

Answers

1. E.g. unexpected; sudden
2. d. an adverb
3. "probably the greatest kids' TV show of all time"
4. E.g. Because they stretched his imagination.
5. E.g. The questions and answers are separated, so it's easy to follow the interview. Each question is in bold, which makes them stand out and shows when a new topic is being introduced.
6. Any appropriate answer. E.g. Yes, because most children like chocolate, so if you found a bar of chocolate then you'd be very pleased. It would also be a nice surprise because you wouldn't be expecting to find it, just like Andy wasn't expecting to get nominated.
7. Any appropriate answer. E.g. Yes, because I love reading and you would get to read lots of books. You would be able to talk about the books with your friends and say what you liked and didn't like about them.

Extra Activities

- As a class, discuss which books pupils have been reading recently. Ask pupils to write a book report about the last book that they have read. It should include who wrote the book and when, a summary of what the book is about and whether they enjoyed it or not.
- Read lines 16-17 aloud to the class. Ask pupils what technique is being used in the name "The Perilous Poozer of Pompelmoose Pass". Get pupils to write their own silly character names using alliteration.
- Get pupils to interview each other about their favourite author. Encourage pupils to listen attentively to the answers their partner gives and to ask them questions based on their answers.
- Invite pupils to write a letter to their favourite author. They should tell the author why they are their favourite, e.g. what they like about their books and how the books make them feel. The pupils could also ask the author some similar questions to those in the extract.
- Ask pupils to pick either "skedaddle", "kerfuffle" or "bamboozle" (line 28). They should look the word up in a dictionary, then draw a magical creature with the characteristics of the definition. E.g. a "skedaddle" might run very fast, a "kerfuffle" might be very messy and a "bamboozle" might confuse its enemies.

Key Stage 2 Comprehension — Year 3

Use this Teacher Book alongside the Targeted Question Book Twos

- To help you find the information you need quickly and easily, the Teacher Book pages are colour-coded to match the colour of the Question Books — purple for Year 3, green for Year 4, orange for Year 5 and turquoise for Year 6.
- The information panel at the top of each page provides the key details about each text. It includes the Targeted Question Book page reference, author or source, genre and cross-curricular links.
- The concise introductions give you all the information you need to present each text to your class, highlighting important facts and concepts that pupils should be aware of before they start reading.
- The answer section for each text contains answers for fact-retrieval questions, and appropriate suggestions and example answers for more complex questions. See page 5 for more about the answers.
- A range of stimulating Extra Activities is provided. These extension activities are all linked to the text and can be used to enhance pupils' understanding of the text, topic and genre. See page 4 for more information about the cross-curricular links in the Extra Activities.

Planning and Delivery

Planning your lessons...

The texts in the Targeted Question Books can be used in any order. The Teacher Book has several useful features that will help you select which texts to use and plan how to incorporate them into your teaching.

The genre charts

- The English National Curriculum requires Key Stage Two pupils to read and discuss a wide range of texts.
- The genre charts on pages 6-9 of this book allow you to easily identify the genre(s) of each text in the Targeted Question Book Twos so you can select the most appropriate text for your lesson.

The cross-curricular subject charts

- The texts in the Targeted Question Books cover a wide range of subject areas, and their varied subject matter offers enormous scope for cross-curricular links and activities.
- The cross-curricular subject charts on pages 10-13 list the cross-curricular links from each Extra Activities section.
- You can use these charts to help you pick out the texts that are best-suited to your class's scheme of work, or to identify texts that will particularly appeal to the interests of your pupils.

	Science	Maths	History	Geography	Art	PE	PSHE	Drama	D&T
The Three Nanny Goats Gruff								performance	designing masks
An Interview with Andy Seed					drawing				
Pioneer Children			the British Empire	migration					
The Reluctant Dragon	animal						prejudice		

The introductions and Extra Activities

- You can use the introductions in the Teacher Book to plan how you will present each text to your class. They provide useful contextual information, and some introductions may also have a starter activity that you can use before pupils start reading the text.
- The Extra Activities will help you to plan which literacy-based activities to incorporate into your teaching and how to build links between reading comprehension tasks and other areas of the curriculum. Many of the Extra Activities are transferable and could also be used alongside different texts and as a foundation for teaching across the whole Key Stage Two curriculum.

Using the texts...

Once you've finished planning, follow these tips to help pupils get to grips with the texts.

Encourage pupils to read carefully

- The introduction to each text in the Targeted Question Books provides useful information about the text and its author or the context in which it was written. This background information is important for pupils' understanding of the text, and pupils should always read it before moving on to the text itself.
- Get pupils to read the introduction and text thoroughly before tackling the questions. Once they are familiar with the content, ask them to read the questions and revisit the text to pick out the key details they need to answer the questions.
- A glossary is provided with some texts, defining the most challenging words. However, pupils should be encouraged to look up any other unfamiliar words in a dictionary and check answers to vocabulary-based questions themselves. Note that as the range contains a variety of genres and authors, some texts use American English spellings. Where appropriate, you may wish to explain this difference to pupils.
- Once pupils have completed the questions, move on to the Extra Activities that you have selected — many of these build on pupils' answers to questions in the Targeted Question Books.

Marking and Monitoring Progress

The Key Stage Two Targeted Comprehension: Set Two includes helpful tools to enable you to check how well your class has understood each text and how their comprehension skills are progressing.

There are ten marks available for each set of questions

Because the questions for each text are marked out of ten, you can easily compare a pupil's performance over the various texts, and see which genres pupils need more practice with. To help you to mark pupils' answers, this Teacher Book provides answers to all of the questions from all four of the Targeted Question Book Twos.

Use your own judgement

- The answers provided in the Teacher Book are intended as a guide only, and you will need to use your own judgement when marking pupils' responses.
- Answers preceded by "E.g." require pupils to offer their own interpretation of the information contained in the text. There is often no 'correct answer', but pupils' answers should be based on the text and go into a similar amount of detail as the sample answer.
- Answers marked "Any appropriate answer" require pupils to offer their own opinions. Again, there is no 'correct answer', and the answers given in the Teacher Book are just suggestions. However, pupils should show a clear understanding of the question and give reasons to support their answer.

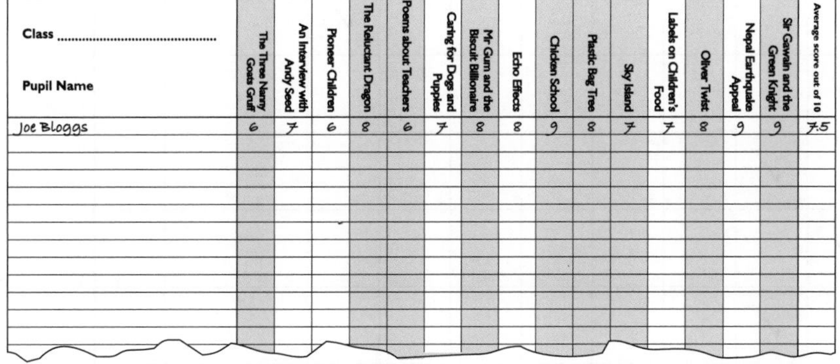

Class .... Pupil Name	The Three Nanny Goats Gruff	An Interview with Andy Seed	Pioneer Children	The Reluctant Dragon	Poems about Teachers	Caring for Dogs and Puppies	Mr Gum and the Biscuit Billionaire	Echo Effects	Chicken School	Plastic Bag Tree	Sky Island	Labels on Children's Food	Oliver Twist	Nepal Earthquake Appeal	Sir Gawain and the Green Knight	Average score out of 10
Joe Bloggs	6	7	6	8	6	7	8	8	9	8	7	7	8	9	9	7.5

Monitoring pupil progress

- Use the four progress charts starting on page 74 to help you keep track of pupils' progress — there is a chart for each year group.
- The progress charts are colour-coded so you can easily distinguish between fiction and non-fiction texts and check which genres your class needs more practice with.

Your turn...

Each Targeted Question Book ends with a 'your turn' activity. See how well pupils' comprehension skills have developed by challenging them to write their own text and construct a series of questions about it. The challenge of writing questions further develops pupils' literacy skills and gives them a new perspective on text comprehension. This activity also provides an opportunity for group or partner work — pupils can swap the texts and questions they have written and attempt to answer each other's questions.

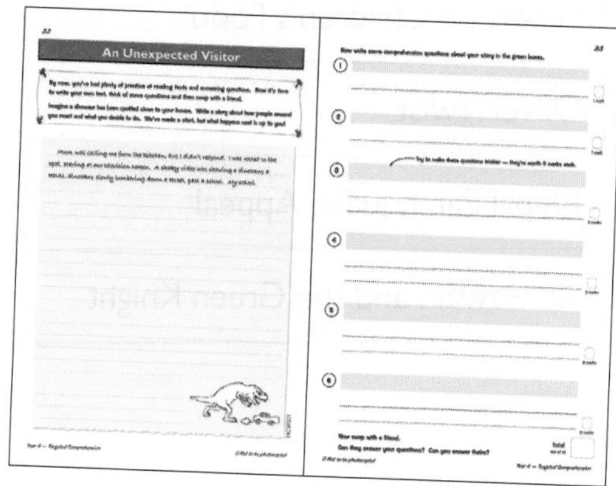

An Unexpected Visitor

Genre Chart — Year 3

	Non-fiction	Fiction	Classic fiction	Autobiography / Memoir	Biography	News article	Playscript	Poetry	Diary	Letter	Myth / Legend
The Three Nanny Goats Gruff							✓				
An Interview with Andy Seed	✓										
Pioneer Children	✓										
The Reluctant Dragon			✓								
Poems about Teachers								✓			
Caring for Dogs and Puppies	✓										
Mr Gum and the Biscuit Billionaire		✓									
Echo Effects	✓										
Chicken School		✓									
Plastic Bag Tree								✓			
Sky Island		✓									
Labels on Children's Food						✓					
Oliver Twist			✓								
Nepal Earthquake Appeal	✓										
Sir Gawain and the Green Knight											✓

Genre Chart — Year 4

	Non-fiction	Fiction	Classic fiction	Autobiography / Memoir	Biography	News article	Playscript	Poetry	Diary	Letter	Myth / Legend
The Diary of a Killer Cat		✓							✓		
Geocaching						✓					
The Dragonsitter's Island		✓									
GRRRR								✓			
Julius Caesar's Goat		✓									
Armoured Dinosaurs	✓										
The Story of Nu Wa											✓
Coram Boy							✓				
An Interview with Tim Peake	✓										
Escape from Germany		✓									
Poems about the Weather								✓			
Wayne Rooney: Captain of England					✓						
The Lion, the Witch and the Wardrobe			✓								
A Letter from Barack Obama										✓	
The Jungle Book			✓								

Genre Chart — Year 5

	Non-fiction	Fiction	Classic fiction	Autobiography / Memoir	Biography	News article	Playscript	Poetry	Diary	Letter	Myth / Legend
Gertrude Ederle	✓										
The Unluckiest Boy in the World		✓									
Baby Birds	✓										
Johnny and the Dead							✓				
Goodnight Mister Tom		✓									
Facts about Hurricanes!	✓										
Poems about Words								✓			
The Oak and the Linden Tree											✓
Cora and the King		✓									
Robot on the Ice						✓					
Candara's Gift		✓									
The Hound of the Baskervilles			✓								
Harambe the Gorilla						✓					
The Highwayman								✓			
Steve Jobs' Biography					✓						

Genre Chart — Year 6

	Non-fiction	Fiction	Classic fiction	Autobiography / Memoir	Biography	News article	Playscript	Poetry	Diary	Letter	Myth / Legend
Talking Turkeys!!								✓			
Pig Heart Boy		✓									
The Story of My Life				✓							
The Lost Diary of Snow White		✓							✓		
The Yellow Train	✓										
David Copperfield			✓								
Edible Cutlery						✓					
The Curse of the Gloamglozer		✓									
Malala Yousafzai					✓						
Poems about World War One								✓			
Moonfleet			✓								
Beowulf the Warrior											✓
Cyber-Bullying						✓					
Romeo and Juliet			✓				✓				
A Letter from a Former Slave										✓	

Cross-Curricular Subject Chart — Year 3

	Science	Maths	History	Geography	Art	PE	PSHE	Drama	D&T
The Three Nanny Goats Gruff								performance	designing masks
An Interview with Andy Seed					drawing				
Pioneer Children			the British Empire	migration					
The Reluctant Dragon	animal behaviour						prejudice		
Poems about Teachers		bar charts						miming	
Caring for Dogs and Puppies	dog breeds								designing a toy
Mr Gum and the Biscuit Billionaire					illustration		boredom		
Echo Effects	sound						technology		
Chicken School					book cover		aspirations; sarcasm		
Plastic Bag Tree	decomposition				illustration		caring for the environment		
Sky Island		analogue clocks		navigation					
Labels on Children's Food	nutrients								packaging; cookery
Oliver Twist			the Victorians		cartoon strip				
Nepal Earthquake Appeal		ordering numbers		Nepal; earthquakes					
Sir Gawain and the Green Knight			oral history; King Arthur		drawing				

Cross-Curricular Subject Chart — Year 4

	Science	Maths	History	Geography	Art	PE	PSHE	Drama / Music	D&T
The Diary of a Killer Cat									product design
Geocaching		coordinates		latitude and longitude					
The Dragonsitter's Island				Scotland; using maps					
GRRRR								performance	
Julius Caesar's Goat			Ancient Rome						
Armoured Dinosaurs	dinosaurs; body armour				illustration				designing a dinosaur
The Story of Nu Wa	the Earth's structure				cartoon strip		myths across cultures		
Coram Boy								performance; classical music	
An Interview with Tim Peake	gravity								designing a patch
Escape from Germany			Nazi Germany				prejudice		
Poems about the Weather					illustration			mood	
Wayne Rooney: Captain of England		measurement				football			
The Lion, the Witch and the Wardrobe	lions				illustration				clay models
A Letter from Barack Obama							social responsibility		
The Jungle Book				India			differences	miming	

Cross-Curricular Subject Chart — Year 5

	Science	Maths	History	Geography	Art	PE	PSHE	Drama	D&T
Gertrude Ederle						water safety; circuit training	gender equality		
The Unluckiest Boy in the World					cartoon strip		loneliness		
Baby Birds	garden birds	statistics							
Johnny and the Dead								script-writing; performance	3D models
Goodnight Mister Tom	nutrition		propaganda; WW2 rationing					role play	
Facts about Hurricanes!				weather	mood boards				
Poems about Words					illustrating imagery			performance	
The Oak and the Linden Tree			Ancient Rome						
Cora and the King							peaceful protests		
Robot on the Ice	meteors			Antarctica					product design
Candara's Gift					fantasy maps				
The Hound of the Baskervilles				UK National Parks					
Harambe the Gorilla	endangered species						animal welfare		
The Highwayman			highwaymen		illustration				
Steve Jobs' Biography							failure		

Cross-Curricular Subject Chart — Year 6

	Science	Maths	History	Geography	Art	PE	PSHE	Drama	D&T
Talking Turkeys!!							reducing waste; animal welfare		
Pig Heart Boy	the heart	line graphs				exercise and heart rate	medical ethics		
The Story of My Life							disability; braille		
The Lost Diary of Snow White									costume and set design
The Yellow Train	circuit diagrams			the Pyrenees	Charles Rennie Mackintosh				
David Copperfield			Victorian Britain					stage directions	
Edible Cutlery	properties of materials	percentages; pie charts					protecting the environment		
The Curse of the Gloamglozer			place names		making a collage				
Malala Yousafzai				rivers			human rights		
Poems about World War One			World War One		modern art		role models		
Moonfleet	astronomy								
Beowulf the Warrior			Anglo-Saxons	Scandinavia				performance	
Cyber-bullying							safety online; bullying	performance	
Romeo and Juliet			Shakespeare		wanted posters			performance	
A Letter From a Former Slave			slavery; abolitionism				modern slavery; freedom		

The Three Nanny Goats Gruff

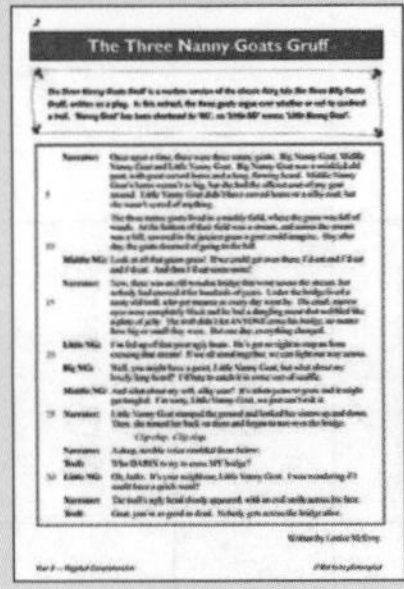

Question Book:
Year 3, pages 2-3

Author / Source:
Louise McEvoy

Genre:
Fiction — playscript

Cross-curricular links:

- D&T (designing masks)
- Drama (performance)

Introduction

The Three Billy Goats Gruff is a fairy tale that originated in Norway. It was first published in the mid-19th century, but many different versions exist today. This extract is from a modern version of the fairy tale, written as a play. This version puts a twist on the traditional story by turning the billy goats into nanny goats. Pupils are introduced to dramatic features such as a narrator, speech and stage directions. When reading this script with pupils, ask them to read out the different parts and encourage them to get into character by using funny voices and intonation where appropriate.

Answers

1. Big Nanny Goat
2. E.g. brave; unafraid; bold; daring
3. E.g. Because it makes it clear how the troll's snout moves.
4. E.g. Because they're not speech, they're stage directions for the sound of the goat's hooves. I think somebody could make the sound using a musical instrument, like a wood block.
5. a. E.g. very loudly b. E.g. That the troll is bad tempered because he's shouting at Little Nanny Goat.
6. Any appropriate answer. E.g. I think she felt angry and upset because she stamped the ground. She might have also been disappointed because her sisters let her down.

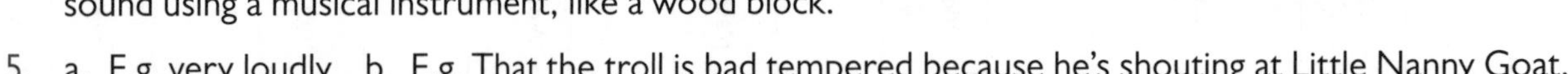

Extra Activities

- As a class, discuss the traditional plot of *The Three Billy Goats Gruff.* Ask pupils why they think the author might have turned the billy goats into nanny goats. Does it change the way they feel about the fairy tale?
- Get pupils to write a letter from Little Nanny Goat's perspective. Their letter should try to persuade Big Nanny Goat and Middle Nanny Goat to cross the bridge and help fight the troll. Encourage pupils to use persuasive techniques like rhetorical questions and emotive language.
- Ask pupils to think of another well-known fairy tale that they would like to turn into a play, e.g. *Jack and the Beanstalk*. Get them to write a short playscript for their chosen fairy tale. Their script can be of a similar length to the extract, and it doesn't have to tell the whole story.
- Get pupils to list the key features of each nanny goat, e.g. Big Nanny Goat is wrinkled, old, with great curved horns and a long beard. Assign each pupil a goat, then ask them to find a photo of a nanny goat with similar features. Pupils should create a mask for their character based on the image they find.
- Split the class into small groups and ask them to prepare a performance of the extract — they could use their masks from the activity above. Ask each group to write down three things that they want to get across about each character through their acting, e.g. the troll should have a loud, deep voice and he should sound rude and threatening.

An Interview with Andy Seed

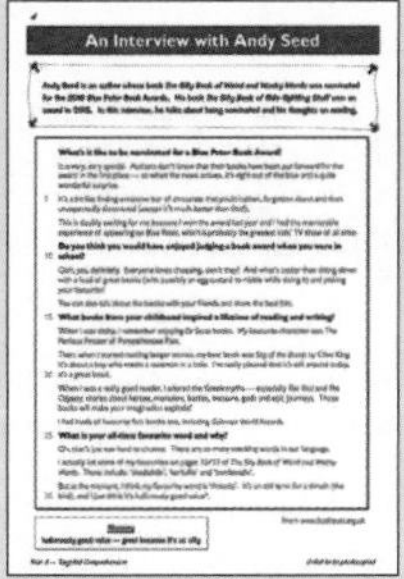

Question Book:
Year 3, pages 4-5

Author / Source:
www.booktrust.org.uk

Genre:
Non-fiction — interview

Cross-curricular links:
- Art (drawing)

Introduction

Andy Seed is a writer of humorous fiction, poetry and non-fiction for children. He also visits schools to encourage children to read for pleasure. This interview was carried out by BookTrust, one of the biggest reading charities in the UK. It aims to inspire a love of reading in both children and adults, and every year the charity donates millions of books to families across the country. Before reading the extract, ask children what their favourite words are and why.

Answers

1. E.g. unexpected; sudden
2. d. an adverb
3. "probably the greatest kids' TV show of all time"
4. E.g. Because they stretched his imagination.
5. E.g. The questions and answers are separated, so it's easy to follow the interview. Each question is in bold, which makes them stand out and shows when a new topic is being introduced.
6. Any appropriate answer. E.g. Yes, because most children like chocolate, so if you found a bar of chocolate then you'd be very pleased. It would also be a nice surprise because you wouldn't be expecting to find it, just like Andy wasn't expecting to get nominated.
7. Any appropriate answer. E.g. Yes, because I love reading and you would get to read lots of books. You would be able to talk about the books with your friends and say what you liked and didn't like about them.

Extra Activities

- As a class, discuss which books pupils have been reading recently. Ask pupils to write a book report about the last book that they have read. It should include who wrote the book and when, a summary of what the book is about and whether they enjoyed it or not.
- Read lines 16-17 aloud to the class. Ask pupils what technique is being used in the name "The Perilous Poozer of Pompelmoose Pass". Get pupils to write their own silly character names using alliteration.
- Get pupils to interview each other about their favourite author. Encourage pupils to listen attentively to the answers their partner gives and to ask them questions based on their answers.
- Invite pupils to write a letter to their favourite author. They should tell the author why they are their favourite, e.g. what they like about their books and how the books make them feel. The pupils could also ask the author some similar questions to those in the extract.
- Ask pupils to pick either "skedaddle", "kerfuffle" or "bamboozle" (line 28). They should look the word up in a dictionary, then draw a magical creature with the characteristics of the definition. E.g. a "skedaddle" might run very fast, a "kerfuffle" might be very messy and a "bamboozle" might confuse its enemies.

Pioneer Children

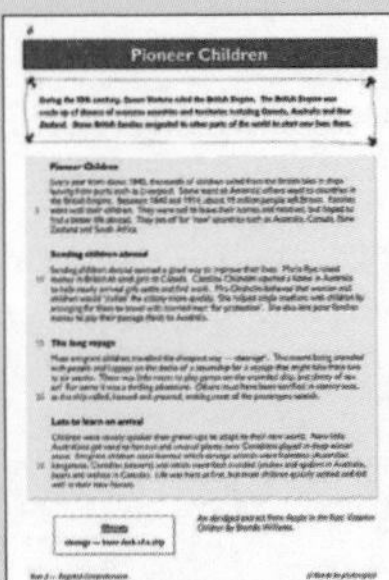

Question Book:
Year 3, pages 6-7

Author / Source:
Brenda Williams

Genre:
Non-fiction — reference text

Cross-curricular links:
- Geography (migration)
- History (the British Empire)

Introduction

Pioneer Children looks at how and why families emigrated from Britain to other corners of the world in the 19th and early 20th centuries. Canada and Australia were two of the most popular destinations. Some children left with their families, but many also travelled by themselves with the help of charities, who believed children would have a better life abroad. Before pupils read the text, make sure they understand what life was like in Victorian England for different people, especially the poor, e.g. child labour and workhouses.

Answers

1. E.g. Because they thought they could find a better life abroad.
2. E.g. Kind, because she lent poor families money so that they could afford to travel to Australia.
3. E.g. exciting; breathtaking; gripping; wondrous
4. Any two from: the hot sun; unusual plants; strange animals
5. Non-fiction. E.g. Because the text gives facts and information about real events.
6. Any appropriate answer. E.g. No, because there wasn't much room to play so I think it would have been boring. OR E.g. Yes, because it would have been an exciting adventure and I could have made friends with the other children on the ship.

Extra Activities

- Ask pupils to imagine they have emigrated to a new country of their choosing. Get them to write a short diary entry about their experiences so far, as well as their thoughts and feelings.
- Ask pupils to write a story about a journey on a boat using some of the details from the text. You could suggest some plot points to the children (e.g. a storm, a seasick passenger and something falling overboard) to help them get started.
- Get pupils to imagine that a child who currently lives abroad is going to emigrate to the pupils' town and join their school. Ask pupils to write a letter to the child explaining what life is like in the UK and the things the child will be able to see and do in their new home town.
- Show pupils a map of the British Empire from a book or the Internet. Encourage pupils to say whether they think the British Empire was powerful and why.
- Linked to the activity above, discuss with pupils why people in Victorian Britain were attracted by the idea of a new life abroad. Show them an old poster or advert which encourages emigration to the British Empire. Ask pupils to explain how the poster or advert tries to persuade people to emigrate, then get them to create their own persuasive posters.

The Reluctant Dragon

Question Book:
Year 3, pages 8-9

Author / Source:
Kenneth Grahame (adapted)

Genre:
Classic fiction — novel extract

Cross-curricular links:

- Science (animal behaviour)
- PSHE (prejudice)

Introduction

The Reluctant Dragon is a parody of the legend of St George and the Dragon. Kenneth Grahame's dragon is an intellectual, who prefers reading and writing poetry to fighting and killing. When St George hears of a dragon living on the South Downs, he goes to kill it — only to find a dragon who doesn't want to fight. St George's reputation is in jeopardy and it's left to the dragon's only friend, a young boy, to protect the dragon and St George's honour. This extract describes the first meeting between the dragon and the Boy. Before reading the extract, make sure that pupils know what the word "reluctant" means.

Answers

1. E.g. Evening because there is a "large moon".
2. a. a verb
3. E.g. Very happy, because the text says that he is "clearly delighted" to have someone to talk to.
4. E.g. happy; good; cheerful; satisfied
5. E.g. He doesn't do all the normal things dragons are expected to do like "chasing knights" and "gobbling damsels". He likes to sleep instead.
6. E.g. Because it makes it sound like the other dragons are very busy and do a lot more than the reluctant dragon.
7. Any appropriate answer. E.g. No, because he seems friendly. He talks to the Boy politely and doesn't seem to do any of the bad things that dragons are famous for.

Extra Activities

- Ask pupils to write a newspaper article reporting the arrival of the dragon. Do pupils think that his arrival would be presented as good news or bad news?
- The dragon in the extract behaves unexpectedly. Get pupils to write a few paragraphs describing what happens next. They should concentrate on continuing to make the dragon's behaviour unexpected.
- As a class, make a list of animals with scary reputations, e.g. sharks, snakes, lions, bears, bats, hyenas. Get pupils to research one of the animals from the list. They should use their research to write a magazine article about their animal, explaining that its scary reputation isn't always deserved.
- Dragons appear in many myths, folktales and stories. As a class, discuss some of these different dragons, e.g. in Chinese culture, in novels such as *The Hobbit* and *Harry Potter.* Ask pupils to research dragons and produce an informative poster about them, including their appearance and characteristics.
- Explain that in the story, the townsfolk are initially afraid of the dragon and want St George to kill it. However, St George and the Boy persuade them that the dragon is harmless and they eventually come to accept it. As a class, discuss the message of the story and the issues it raises. E.g. the dangers of making judgements based on appearances and prejudice, and the difficulties of being different.

Poems about Teachers

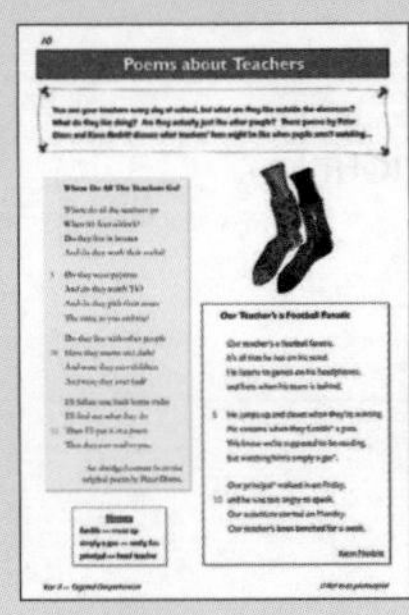

Question Book:
Year 3, pages 10-11

Author / Source:
Peter Dixon
Kenn Nesbitt

Genre:
Poetry

Cross-curricular links:
- Drama (miming)
- Maths (bar charts)

Introduction

Peter Dixon is a poet and a painter. He performs at schools and festivals, and one of his poetry collections, *The Colour of My Dreams,* has been turned into a music album. Kenn Nesbitt is a popular and prolific American children's poet. It's worth noting that Nesbitt's poem is about American football. However, interpreting 'football' as 'soccer' doesn't detract from the overall meaning of the poem. The two poems offer good points of comparison on subject matter, rhyme scheme and language.

Answers

1. TV and me
2. By following them home.
3. E.g. To show that the narrator is curious about teachers' lives.
4. b. worries
5. E.g. The head teacher came into the pupils' classroom and was angry because the teacher was listening to football instead of teaching. The teacher has been suspended, so the class will be taught by someone else.
6. E.g. I think both poems suggest that teachers are just like most people. They do normal things like wash their socks and support football teams.
7. Any appropriate answer. E.g. I prefer Nesbitt's poem because it made me laugh. It's funny that the teacher gets told off by the head teacher. Normally it's the children who get into trouble. OR E.g. I prefer Dixon's poem because it made me think about what my teachers might be like outside school.

Extra Activities

- Read Dixon's poem to the class and ask pupils to underline any words that they think rhyme. Then read it again and ask pupils to join in on the words that they've picked out. Repeat the process with Nesbitt's poem. As a class, discuss whether the poems' rhyme schemes are similar or different.
- Ask pupils to write a verse of a poem in a similar style to Nesbitt's, swapping the idea of a football fanatic for a different personality trait. You could suggest some possible titles to the class, e.g. "Our Friend's a Food Fanatic".
- Ask pupils to rewrite Nesbitt's poem as a story.
- Split the class into two groups and assign one poem to each group. Get pupils to create mimes for the actions, nouns and emotions in each poem, e.g. for the first two lines of Dixon's poem, pupils could march on the spot, then tap their wrists and hold up four fingers to indicate four o'clock. Encourage volunteers from each group to perform their mimes as you re-read the poems to the class.
- Ask pupils to conduct a survey asking teachers what they like to do outside school. Get them to collect their data as a tally chart and then put their findings into a bar chart.

Caring for Dogs and Puppies

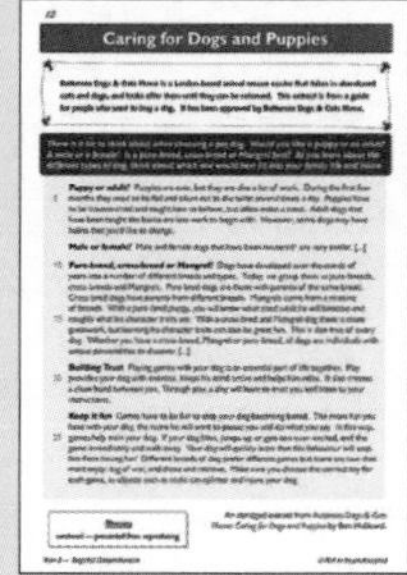

Question Book:
Year 3, pages 12-13

Author / Source:
Ben Hubbard

Genre:
Non-fiction — reference text

Cross-curricular links:
- Science (dog breeds)
- D&T (designing a toy)

Introduction

This family-friendly guide was written to advise parents and children on how to care for dogs and puppies. Its clear layout and simple language create an informative text that is very accessible for young readers. This extract focuses on how owners can find a suitable dog for their needs. Before reading the text, ask if any pupils have a dog and get them to tell the class about it, e.g. its name, what it looks like and its personality.

Answers

1. E.g. By putting it in a separate, darker-coloured box. The font is also a different colour to the main text and is in italics.
2. E.g. You will have a good idea what character traits a pure-bred puppy will develop. This is a good thing because it helps you to choose a dog that suits your personality.

3. E.g. individual; one of a kind; different
4. c. It improves your relationship with your dog.
5. E.g. To give advice to people who are thinking of buying a dog, so they make the best choice. I think the charity wants to make sure that dogs get the best start in their new home.
6. Any appropriate answer. E.g. A puppy, because I would enjoy working hard to train it and look after it. OR E.g. An adult dog, because it would be easier to manage and my parents wouldn't let me have a dog that wasn't housetrained.

Extra Activities

- Discuss the text as a class. Did pupils learn anything new from it? Do they think the guide is useful? Encourage pupils to think of ways to improve it further, e.g. by including images to make it more attractive, or by giving examples of pure-bred, cross-bred and Mongrel dogs.
- Get pupils to draw a table listing the pros and cons of getting a puppy. Pupils should come up with their own ideas as well as referring to the extract. Then get pupils to write a letter to their parents arguing either for or against getting a puppy. Encourage them to use persuasive techniques, e.g. lists of three.
- Give pupils some phrases to do with dogs, e.g. in the doghouse, make a dog's dinner of something, dog-eared, it's a dog's life, call off the dogs, gone to the dogs, let sleeping dogs lie. Ask pupils to guess the meaning of each one. Encourage them to share their ideas, then go through the answers as a class.
- Give pupils a list of different breeds of dog, e.g. Golden Retriever, Springer Spaniel, Rottweiler, Greyhound, Labrador and Newfoundland. Ask each pupil to research one of the breeds on the list and use a computer to design a profile for it based on their findings. Pupils should find out their dog's country of origin, its physical features (e.g. weight, height), common personality traits and what activities it enjoys.
- Ask pupils to design their own dog toy for either "tug of war" or "chase and retrieve". Pupils should draw and label their design with essential information, e.g. the materials to be used, the size of the toy, any noises it makes. They should also think carefully about the shape of their toy and explain their choice.

Mr Gum and the Biscuit Billionaire

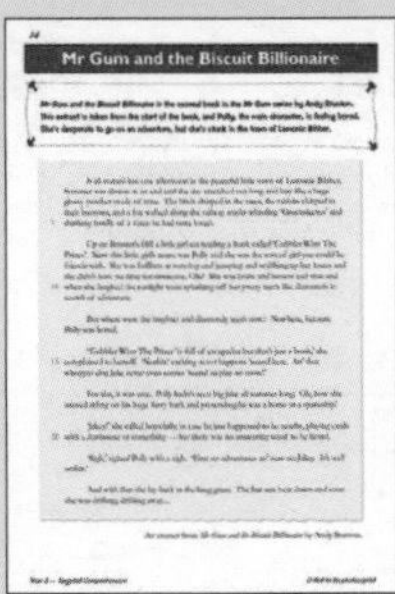

Question Book:
Year 3, pages 14-15

Author / Source:
Andy Stanton

Genre:
Fiction — novel extract

Cross-curricular links:
- Art (illustration)
- PSHE (boredom)

Introduction

Mr Gum and the Biscuit Billionaire is the sequel to *You're a Bad Man, Mr Gum!*, which was Andy Stanton's first book. The *Mr Gum* series has now been published in over 30 countries and has won several awards, including the Roald Dahl Funny Prize. The books are set in a weird and wonderful imaginary world, where animals can talk and some people are only a few centimetres tall. This extract introduces pupils to this world and to the book's heroine, Polly.

Answers

1. E.g. The animals aren't behaving normally. For example, the fox is acting like a human and the rabbits are making bird noises.
2. E.g. Because nothing exciting happens in the town. OR E.g. Because big Jake hasn't been around.
3. b. adventures
4. E.g. Some words like "'round" and "an'" are missing letters. The author did this to show that Polly has an accent which means that she doesn't always pronounce the start and the end of her words.
5. E.g. To show that Polly is feeling bored.
6. E.g. Yes, because she's "brave", "honest" and "true". She also likes having adventures, so I think she would be fun to play with.
7. Any appropriate answer. E.g. Yes, because it seems like Polly is about to have an adventure. She seems like a fun character and I want to know what happens to her.

Extra Activities

- Ask pupils to continue the story by writing about something exciting that happens to Polly.
- Stanton uses unusual similes in his writing. Introduce children to similes and explain why writers use them. Discuss the similes in the extract, e.g. "like a huge glossy panther made of time" and "the sunlight went splashing off her pretty teeth like diamonds in search of adventure", and the effect that they have on the reader. Get pupils to write their own similes to describe one of their friends.
- The extract describes animals doing unusual things, for example, the fox is walking and whistling. Get pupils to write a few sentences about animals acting in unexpected ways, e.g. a cat barking.
- Ask pupils to design an illustration for the extract. They should try to capture the calm and peaceful setting, as well as Polly's boredom and frustration. Encourage them to include details from the extract in their illustration, such as the birds and rabbits.
- Discuss boredom with the class. Do they ever get bored? When are they most likely to get bored? How do they feel when they are bored? How do they deal with boredom? Could they do more to stop themselves getting bored?

Echo Effects

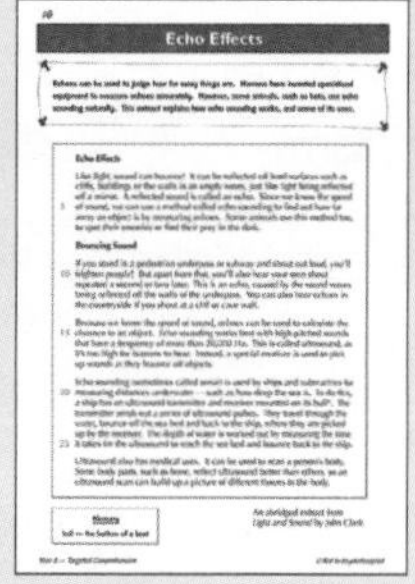

Question Book:
Year 3, pages 16-17

Author / Source:
John Clark

Genre:
Non-fiction — reference text

Cross-curricular links:

- Science (sound)
- PSHE (technology)

Introduction

Light and Sound is part of the *Mad About Science* series, written by John Clark. The series is designed to help Key Stage Two pupils develop an understanding of and interest in science. This extract looks at echoes and how they are used in sonar and ultrasound. Before reading the extract, ask pupils to suggest some places that are good for creating echoes. Ask them if these places have anything in common with each other.

Answers

1. E.g. Because it helps readers to imagine how echoes work. Most people will have seen how light reflects off mirrors, so this makes it easier to understand how sound reflects off hard surfaces.
2. To spot their enemies and to find their prey in the dark.
3. c. a verb
4. E.g. Ships send out ultrasound pulses and crew members record how long the pulses take to reach the seabed and bounce back up. This tells them how far away the seabed is.
5. E.g. Because they are hard.
6. Any appropriate answer. E.g. I think using ultrasound to scan a person's body is more useful because it can help to detect important medical problems. Measuring the depth of the sea doesn't help ill people.

Extra Activities

- Ask pupils to summarise the information from the third paragraph.
- Discuss the features of this text that show it is a non-fiction extract. Do pupils prefer to read fiction or non-fiction texts? Encourage them to give reasons for their preferences.
- Split the class into small groups. Ask each group to write a presentation about an animal which uses echo sounding, such as bats, dolphins or whales. Pupils should present their findings to the rest of the class. Encourage pupils to work on their presentation skills by talking clearly, and at a good volume and speed. Encourage the rest of the class to develop their listening skills by sitting quietly and thinking of a thoughtful question to ask at the end of each presentation.
- Ask pupils to re-read the fourth paragraph. Get them to draw a diagram explaining how sonar works, using their answer to question 4 in the Question Book to help them. Encourage them to label their diagrams with the technical terms mentioned in the extract.
- Ask pupils to share their answers to question 6 in the Question Book and then initiate a class discussion on technology. Do pupils think that the most important pieces of technology are the ones that help to keep humans healthy (e.g. thermometers and X-rays)? If pupils could only take five pieces of technology to a desert island, what would they take?

Chicken School

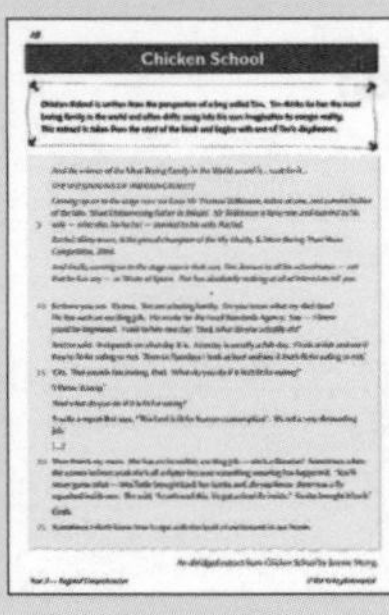

Question Book:
Year 3, pages 18-19

Author / Source:
Jeremy Strong

Genre:
Fiction — novel extract

Cross-curricular links:

- PSHE (aspirations; sarcasm)
- Art (book cover)

Introduction

Jeremy Strong is an English author who is famous for his funny children's stories. He also writes joke books, quizzes and puzzles. He's written over 100 books, including *Chicken School*, which was first published in 2004. Sarcastic and self-deprecating, the narration of the main character, Tim, is guaranteed to make most pupils laugh. Tim thinks he has the most boring family in the world and spends his days at school dreaming up exciting stories in which he features as the hero.

Answers

1. E.g. To show that it's an announcement and that it's being said really loudly.
2. E.g. No, because in Tim's daydream he says that he has no friends and is known as "Waste of Space".
3. E.g. By putting them in italics.
4. Tim
5. E.g. No, because the extract is all about how he finds his family boring.
6. E.g. That she is excited and can't sit still.
7. Any appropriate answer. E.g. No, because Tim's parents don't have exciting jobs, so living with them would be boring. OR E.g. Yes, because Tim has a good sense of humour. I think that we would get on well and he would make me laugh.

Extra Activities

- Explain to the class what sarcasm is. Ask pupils to pick out examples of sarcasm from the extract (e.g. "He has such an exciting job"). Discuss why the author uses sarcasm and the effect it has on the reader. Do they find it funny? What other techniques do authors use to make their writing funny?
- Ask pupils to write a short story about the "My Hobby Is More Boring Than Yours Competition". They should write about the champion and their winning hobby, as well as the hobbies of the runners-up.
- Jeremy Strong uses alliteration, e.g. "Witkinsons of Widdlingwall". Remind the class about how to use alliteration. Discuss why some authors and poets might use it. Ask students to come up with their own alliterative phrases to do with place names, e.g. the parakeets of Paddington.
- With the whole class, discuss whether pupils think that Tim's parents' jobs sound boring. Ask pupils to identify a job that they would like to do as an adult. They should research their chosen job and then write a paragraph explaining what it involves and why they would like to do it.
- Sarcasm can be funny, but it can also be hurtful. Split the class into groups and ask them to discuss sarcasm and how it can make people feel.
- Invite pupils to design a cartoon-style front cover for this book, based on the information in the extract and in the introduction.

Plastic Bag Tree

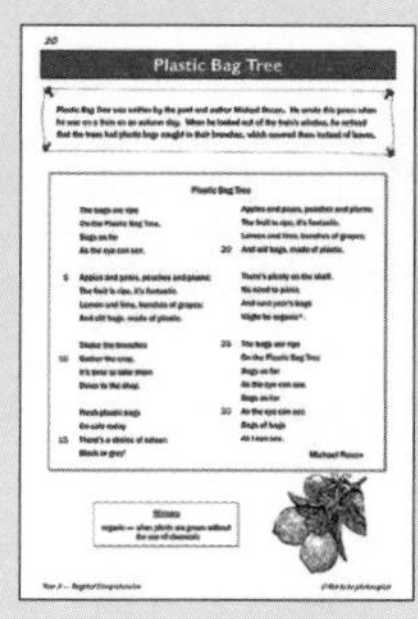

Question Book:
Year 3, pages 20-21

Author / Source:
Michael Rosen

Genre:
Poetry

Cross-curricular links:
- Art (illustration)
- Science (decomposition)
- PSHE (caring for the environment)

Introduction

Michael Rosen is an English writer and poet. Pupils may already have read some of his most famous works, including *We're Going on a Bear Hunt*. Rosen was Children's Laureate between 2007 and 2009, and focused on making poetry more accessible in schools. He writes mainly for children, and his fiction and poetry are well known for their humour and fun use of language. *Plastic Bag Tree* is a light-hearted poem with a serious message about the environment.

Answers

1. tree and see
2. E.g. Yes, because the poet says there are "bags as far as the eye can see".
3. E.g. To make the plastic bags fall off the tree.
4. ripe and fresh e.g. To make the plastic bags sound like fruit.
5. E.g. fret; be alarmed
6. E.g. It's used once to mean 'a lot of' and once to mean the noun 'bags'.
7. E.g. I think Michael Rosen is saying that littering is bad and it is a big problem because there are "bags as far as the eye can see". He pretends the bags are like fruit, but it makes the reader realise that it's not natural that plastic bags are found on trees.

Extra Activities

- Discuss the form of the poem with the class. Ask pupils to look for patterns, e.g. the lengths of the stanzas and words that rhyme. As a class, decide whether you think the poem is regular or irregular.
- Explain to the class what imagery is. Get pupils to identify imagery used in the poem and ask them why they think Michael Rosen chose to write about plastic bags growing on trees. Does it seem like a natural or unnatural idea? Do pupils think that it would look nice? Ask pupils to look at their answers to question 7 in the Question Book. How does the imagery in the poem help to reinforce its message?
- Get pupils to use details from the poem to create an illustration for it.
- Ask pupils to design a poster encouraging people not to litter. They should concentrate on using layout, language and pictures to make the poster as persuasive as they can.
- Introduce pupils to the terms biodegradable and non-biodegradable. Discuss with the class why it's important to reuse or recycle non-biodegradable waste. Give the class a list of objects and ask them to decide whether each one is biodegradeable or non-biodegradable, e.g. banana skins and plastic bottles.
- Explain that the government has brought in a plastic bag charge to try to reduce the number of plastic bags that are thrown away each year. Split the class into pairs. One pupil in each pair should argue in favour of the charge and the other should argue against it.

Sky Island

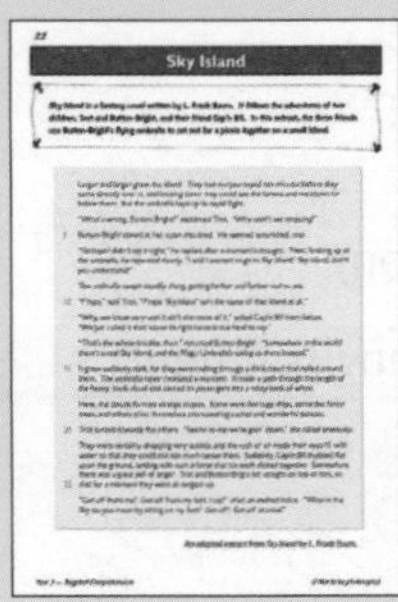

Question Book:
Year 3, pages 22-23

Author / Source:
L. Frank Baum (adapted)

Genre:
Fiction — novel extract

Cross-curricular links:
- Geography (navigation)
- Maths (analogue clocks)

Introduction

L. Frank Baum is best known as the author of the *Oz* books, the popular children's series which inspired the 1939 film *The Wizard of Oz*. His unmistakable creativity and sense of adventure are evident in his children's novel *Sky Island*, which was published in 1912. The novel centres on three friends who are carried away by a flying umbrella to a magical island in the sky. Before introducing the class to this extract, ask pupils to look at the title and predict what it's going to be about.

Answers

1. E.g. Because they asked for 'Sky Island' instead of using the real name of the island they wanted to go to.
2. E.g. To help you to imagine what Trot's accent sounds like.
3. E.g. They're shaped like objects such as trees, palaces and ships.
4. a. E.g. nervously; worriedly; fearfully; uneasily
   b. E.g. Because she doesn't know where they're going to land. She might also be worried about getting hurt when they land because they're going down very fast.
5. E.g. Because there is so much confusion when the umbrella suddenly lands that it's impossible to tell where everyone has landed and who is yelling.
6. Any appropriate answer. E.g. Yes, because it would be exciting. The umbrella goes quickly and you'd get to fly very high in the clouds. OR E.g. No, because it could be dangerous. The umbrella doesn't sound very easy to control and I think you could get hurt easily.

Extra Activities

- Ask pupils to write the next paragraph of the story. It should include a description of the person who appears at the end of the extract. Pupils should look for clues in the extract to help them, e.g. "yell of anger" (line 24) and "excited voice" (line 26).
- As a class, discuss how Trot might be feeling at different points in the extract. Then ask pupils to create a wordbank for her character. The words should describe how she's feeling, (e.g. excited, scared, nervous, regretful) and her personality (e.g. brave, calm, adventurous, fun).
- Ask pupils to imagine that someone was spotted using an umbrella to fly above their home town. Get pupils to write a newspaper article reporting the sighting. Encourage them to include details like the time of the sighting, an eyewitness account and the reaction of local people.
- Explain to pupils that it is possible to navigate using the position of the Sun. Ask them to draw a clock and get them to add the time onto their drawings (the time doesn't have to be exact, it just has to be the right hour). Outside, ask pupils to lay their drawings on the ground, lining up the little hand with the direction of the sun. The mid-point between the little hand and the number 12 will show them which direction is south.

Labels on Children's Food

Labels on Children's Food

Parents confused by labels on food for children

Question Book:
Year 3, pages 24-25

Author / Source:
www.independent.co.uk

Genre:
Non-fiction — news article

Cross-curricular links:
- D&T (packaging; cookery)
- Science (nutrients)

Introduction

Parents often buy food aimed specifically at children, assuming that they are making healthy choices. However, this article explains that this isn't always the case. Many products aimed at children contain high levels of sugar and salt or a long list of artificial additives. Identifying which products are healthy and which ones aren't isn't easy, especially when faced with confusing packaging.

Answers

1. E.g. prevented; hindered; restricted
2. Any two from: many food products contain lots of artificial additives; there are confusing health claims on the packaging; parents don't know what many of the ingredients are.
3. E.g. Making something from the very beginning without using any ready-made products.
4. E.g. By looking carefully at labels and by making a lot of food from scratch.
5. c. to make as much money as possible.
6. E.g. The text is in columns and there is a big headline.
7. Any appropriate answer. E.g. I think it's more important that food tastes good. If it doesn't taste good then you won't enjoy it, and it's important to enjoy your food. OR E.g. I think that it's more important that food is healthy. An unhealthy diet might make you unwell.

Extra Activities

- With the whole class, discuss pupils' answers to question 7 in the Question Book, encouraging them to expand on the answers they wrote down. Split the class into two groups and hold a debate about whether it's more important that food is healthy or that it tastes good.
- Ask pupils to write a speech for a school assembly which will persuade other pupils to eat more healthily. Pupils may want to research some facts and statistics about healthy eating to back up their arguments.
- Get pupils to design packaging for a healthy food product aimed at children, e.g. carrot sticks. Remind pupils to think carefully about the pictures and colours that they choose to show that it's a healthy product and to make it appealing to young people.
- Explain to pupils that different foods contain different nutrients, which have special jobs around the body. Discuss the importance of nutrients like iron, protein and vitamin C.
- Introduce pupils to 'the eatwell plate', a picture guide that shows which foods need to be eaten and in what quantities to have a healthy, well-balanced diet. Get the pupils to plan a healthy meal based on the eatwell plate.
- Hold a simple cooking lesson where pupils learn how to make healthy snacks, e.g. fruit kebabs, homemade popcorn and tuna wraps.

Oliver Twist

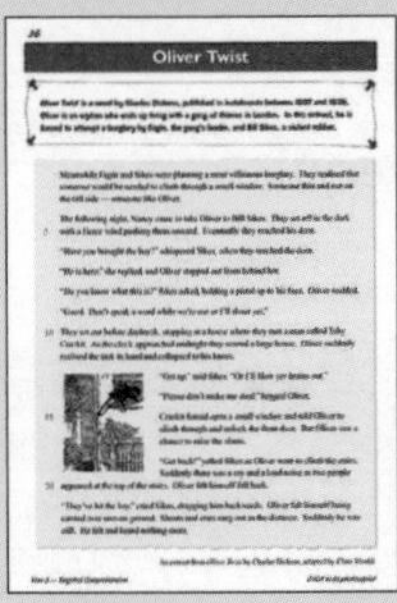

Question Book:
Year 3, pages 26-27

Author / Source:
Charles Dickens
Adapted by Chris Mould

Genre:
Classic fiction — novel extract

Cross-curricular links:
- Art (cartoon strip)
- History (the Victorians)

Introduction

Oliver Twist was Charles Dickens' second novel. Although it was originally written for adults, this version by Chris Mould is one of many adaptations suitable for younger readers. The novel is set in London in the mid-19th century. After the events in this extract, Bill Sikes runs away from the house and abandons Oliver, who is injured, in a nearby ditch. Oliver manages to crawl out of the ditch and knock on the door of the house for help. The family there take him in and nurse him back to health.

Answers

1. E.g. Because they need someone short and thin to climb through a small window.
2. E.g. finally; at last
3. E.g. Because he is scared.
4. E.g. Because there wouldn't be many people around when it was dark.
5. b. an adjective
6. E.g. Two people appear at the top of the stairs and Oliver is injured.
7. Any appropriate answer. E.g. I think Oliver is honest because he says that he doesn't want to steal. He also tries to let the people in the house know that they're being burgled.
8. Any appropriate answer. E.g. I think that they will get away, but that Oliver will become very ill because he's been badly hurt. Bill Sikes might also punish Oliver for disobeying him.

Extra Activities

- The extract uses personification to describe the weather (e.g. "a fierce wind"). Explain what personification is, then ask pupils to write their own descriptions of different types of weather using personification.
- Get pupils to write a newspaper article about the break-in. Remind them to include common features of newspaper articles, such as a headline, columns, a picture and a caption.
- Ask the class to imagine that Oliver is on trial for burglary. Split the class into two groups, making one group the prosecution and the other the defence. Ask the prosecution to come up with reasons why Oliver should be punished and the defence to explain why he shouldn't. Both groups should present their arguments to a 'judge', who should decide on Oliver's verdict.
- Ask children to make a cartoon strip of the events in the extract. Encourage them to focus on communicating Oliver's emotions in their drawings, e.g. feeling threatened and scared.
- Split the class into groups and give each group one topic to research about life in Victorian times, e.g. workhouses, prisons or schools. Get the groups to present their findings to the rest of the class.

Nepal Earthquake Appeal

Question Book:
Year 3, pages 28-29

Author / Source:
www.savethechildren.org.uk

Genre:
Non-fiction — information text

Cross-curricular links:

- Geography (Nepal; earthquakes)
- Maths (ordering numbers)

Introduction

The earthquake that hit Nepal in April 2015 killed thousands of people and left thousands more injured. The international community played an important part in rescue operations after the earthquake, and charities like Save the Children helped to provide disaster relief. This extract from a report by Save the Children explains how donations and resources were used to provide help in the aftermath. Before pupils read the article, show them some pictures of the devastation caused by the earthquake.

Answers

1. E.g. To give them shelter because their houses were flattened.
2. nearly 29,000
3. Any two from: shelter materials and vital household items have been distributed; emergency mobile health units have gone to villages; health clinics have been set up; thousands of hygiene kits have been given out.
4. c. essential
5. E.g. Because it meant a lot to see a new life come into the world amongst so much death and destruction.
6. E.g. To let people who donated money know how they made a difference in Nepal. They might also have written it to persuade other people to donate money to Save the Children.
7. Any appropriate answer. E.g. Yes, because charities like Save the Children make a big difference. In Nepal, they helped thousands of people. Without donations, charities wouldn't be able to help as many people.

Extra Activities

- As a class, discuss what it would be like to live without shelter, running water, electricity etc. Ask pupils to write a diary entry describing how it might feel to live without these things.
- Ask the class if they know where Nepal is or if they can find it on a map. Then split the class into groups and give each group a topic on Nepal to research, e.g. geography, history, culture, work, religion. Ask each group to make a leaflet which summarises the key facts about their topic, using features like subheadings and bullet points to present their findings clearly.
- Introduce pupils to 'tectonic plates' and 'faults'. Explain that earthquakes happen when tectonic plates rub together. Get a world map from the Internet which shows fault lines. With the class, look at recent serious earthquakes and mark them on the map, e.g. India in 2004, Japan in 2011.
- Explain that the strength of an earthquake is measured using a scale that goes from 1-10. Earthquakes that measure 1 on the scale are very small and earthquakes that measure 10 are extreme. Give each pupil a list of earthquakes and their magnitudes. Ask pupils to put them in order of strength, from weakest to strongest.

Italy, 2009 — 6.3
Pakistan, 2005 — 7.6
New Zealand, 2016 — 5.8
Argentina, 2006 — 6.2
Laos, 2007 — 6.3
Chile, 2010 — 8.8
Falkland Islands, 2013 — 7.0
Puerto Rico, 2016 — 2.7

Sir Gawain and the Green Knight

Question Book:
Year 3, pages 30-31

Author / Source:
Michael Morpurgo

Genre:
Legend

Cross-curricular links:
- History (oral history; King Arthur)
- Art (drawing)

Introduction

Sir Gawain and the Green Knight is a legend written in verse which dates from the 14th century. There have been numerous different versions of the story, and this interpretation was written by Michael Morpurgo in 2004. Although Morpurgo's version is written in prose, the plot is faithful to the original story and uses engaging language to capture the reader's imagination. Before they begin, children might benefit from learning a little about King Arthur and the Knights of the Round Table.

Answers

1. E.g. That no one can eat until someone tells a new story.
2. E.g. Stories that aren't true.
3. roaring OR rattle OR clatter
4. E.g. They are thick and strong.
5. E.g. To show how strange it is that the giant is green and to create a strong picture in the reader's head.
6. a. E.g. A stranger entering the hall and challenging him.
   b. E.g. Because the Green Knight appears straight after Arthur stops speaking. The timing is spooky.
7. E.g. Scared, because his appearance is very frightening, and the expression on his face "struck terror into every heart".

Extra Activities

- Discuss with the class how Morpurgo creates tension in the extract. Highlight his use of onomatopoeia at the start of the second paragraph and in the fearsome description of the giant. Ask pupils to write their own short paragraph about a monster using similar techniques.
- This legend was originally written in verse. As a class, summarise the key events in the text. Get pupils to use this summary to write a poem which tells the same story as the extract. Make it clear that pupils don't have to make their poems rhyme, but they can use rhymes if they wish.
- Ask pupils to write a diary entry from the perspective of one of the knights. They should explore what the knight thought when he heard the noises outside and how he felt when he saw the creature.
- Legends are traditionally passed down orally. Split the class into pairs and ask pupils to retell the story of the extract without looking at the text. In their pairs, ask students to discuss how similar the version they told was to the original. As a class, discuss what their findings suggest about stories passed down orally.
- Get pupils to use the extract to draw an illustration of The Green Knight. Ask pupils to compare their drawings and discuss the similarities and differences between them. Are they surprised that the same text can inspire different artistic interpretations?
- Make sure pupils understand that no one is sure if King Arthur really existed. Ask pupils to research the legend of Arthur and make a storyboard of the main events of his life and how he became King.

The Diary of a Killer Cat

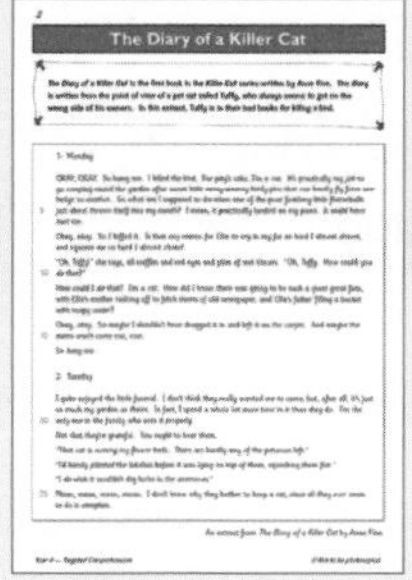

Question Book:
Year 4, pages 2-3

Author / Source:
Anne Fine

Genre:
Fiction — novel extract

Cross-curricular links:
- D&T (product design)

Introduction

Anne Fine is a former Children's Laureate and a prolific writer for children and young adults. She has won several prestigious awards, including the Carnegie Medal. Pupils may be familiar with some of her other works, such as *Bill's New Frock*. This extract from *The Diary of a Killer Cat* is written from the perspective of a cat called Tuffy and offers an amusing take on the relationship between a pet and its owners. Tuffy's dry and witty first-person narrative gives a clear insight into his personality. Before pupils read the text, show them the title and ask what they think it is going to be about.

Answers

1. E.g. It has subheadings which split the text up into different days of the week.
2. E.g. Very sad. She cried a lot when she found out.
3. E.g. To clean up the stains that the bird left on the carpet.
4. E.g. They held a funeral in the garden for the bird.
5. E.g. To show that the family complains about Tuffy all the time.
6. E.g. So that they stand out from the rest of the text and are said with more stress when you read them.
7. Any appropriate answer. E.g. No, because he's a cat and it's natural for cats to kill birds. They can't help it. OR E.g. Yes, because Tuffy can obviously think for himself and knows what he did was wrong. For example, he says, "So maybe I shouldn't have dragged it in and left it on the carpet".

Extra Activities

- As a class, discuss whether the predictions pupils made before reading the text were correct. Are they surprised by Tuffy's character? Do they think it's appropriate to call him a 'killer cat'? Why do they think Fine used this phrase in the book's title?
- Explain what exaggeration is and get pupils to find examples of it in the extract. Ask pupils to write their own diary entry which starts in a similar way to the extract, e.g. 'OKAY, OKAY. So hang me. I ate the roast chicken. For pity's sake, I'm a *dog*!' Encourage pupils to use exaggeration in their writing.
- In the extract, Tuffy describes birds as "feathery little flutterballs". Explain that "flutterballs" is a nonsense word and discuss how the word reminds the reader of birds. Challenge pupils to come up with their own nonsense words to describe animals, e.g. a 'wagbottom' for a dog.
- Get pupils to write a letter of apology from Tuffy to the bird's family, explaining what happened. Make sure they include the layout features of a formal letter (e.g. addresses and the date).
- Ask pupils to design a garden bird feeder. Encourage them to think about how they can protect the feeder from cats, e.g. it could be enclosed in a cage or suspended from a tall metal pole. Pupils should draw an annotated diagram of their design and explain it to the class.

Geocaching

Geocaching

Challenge yourself with a GPS-assisted treasure hunt

Question Book:
Year 4, pages 4-5

Author / Source:
www.telegraph.co.uk

Genre:
Non-fiction — news article

Cross-curricular links:

- Maths (coordinates)
- Geography (latitude and longitude)

Introduction

In 2000, the US military altered its GPS settings, which made GPS technology much more accurate for the general public. An American, Dave Ulmer, tested this accuracy by hiding a black bucket near Beavercreek, Oregon, and sharing the coordinates online with other GPS enthusiasts. People enjoyed looking for this 'hidden treasure', and began to hide caches of their own. Today, there are more than 2.8 million geocaches hidden all over the world. Before pupils read the extract, ask if any of them have been geocaching before.

Answers

1. E.g. Because people searching for caches and the goodies inside them are like pirates hunting for treasure.
2. adventure
3. Any two from: a toy soldier, a cheap pendant, a logbook.
4. E.g. I think the author likes geocaching because they write in a persuasive way. For example, they say it is a "great family activity".
5. E.g. It has a large headline and is written in columns. It also includes a picture with a caption.
6. Any appropriate answer. E.g. You have to have the right technology to be able to go geocaching. People who don't have GPS-enabled devices can't take part.

Extra Activities

- Get pupils to produce a poster persuading people to try geocaching. They should use the information in the extract and present it in an appealing and engaging way.
- Discuss pupils' answers to question 5 in the Question Book, then ask them to write their own newspaper article giving advice on how to be a successful geocacher. Pupils should think about what skills a good geocacher might need, useful equipment to take, practical clothing etc.
- Ask pupils to write a short story about something exciting that happens to them while they are out geocaching, e.g. they might get lost or stumble upon something that they weren't expecting.
- Get each pupil to draw a coordinate grid, labelling the x and y axis from 1 to 10. Ask them to secretly mark the location of buried treasure at three points on their grid and write down the coordinates of each location. In pairs, pupils should take it in turns to guess the coordinates of their partner's buried treasure. Pupils should mark each guess that their partner makes on their grid with a cross. The first pupil in the pair to locate all of their partner's buried treasure wins.
- Give pupils a map of the world with lines of longitude and latitude marked at 15° intervals. Explain how longitude and latitude can be used to pinpoint specific locations and challenge pupils to find various locations on their maps.

The Dragonsitter's Island

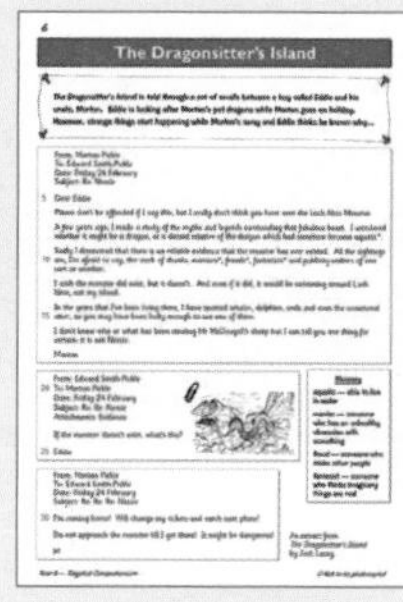
The Dragonsitter's Island

Question Book:
Year 4, pages 6-7

Author / Source:
Josh Lacey

Genre:
Fiction — novel extract

Cross-curricular links:

- Geography (Scotland; using maps)

Introduction

The Dragonsitter's Island is the fourth book in Josh Lacey's *Dragonsitter* series. Lacey is a British author who has written dozens of books for children. The *Dragonsitter* books follow the adventures of Eddie, his Uncle Morton and Uncle Morton's pet dragons. They are written as a series of emails between Eddie and Uncle Morton. In this extract, Eddie writes to tell his uncle that he has seen the Loch Ness Monster. Before reading the extract, make sure pupils are aware of the legend of Nessie.

Answers

1. E.g. The text is split into boxes, and each one starts with the date and the subject, which you'd normally find at the start of an email. Each box ends with the character's name or initial on a separate line.
2. E.g. Proof that you can trust.
3. Any appropriate answer. E.g. So that they become famous.
4. E.g. Someone or something has been stealing Mr McDougall's sheep.
5. E.g. He makes his sentences shorter, which makes it sound like Morton's in a rush. He also uses lots of exclamation marks.
6. Any appropriate answer. E.g. Because he's really interested in the Loch Ness Monster and wants to see it.
7. Any appropriate answer. E.g. I wouldn't believe them because I don't think monsters are real. I'd tell them that they'd imagined it.

Extra Activities

- Ask pupils to write an email from Uncle Morton to a friend as he's flying back to meet Eddie. Pupils should focus on how Morton is feeling about the sighting of the Loch Ness Monster and what he hopes to do when he gets back to his island.
- Ask pupils to imagine they're on holiday and see a monster. They should write a story about their encounter.
- Get pupils to research the legend of the Loch Ness Monster. Ask them to produce an information leaflet about the legend for tourists visiting Loch Ness. They should include useful information, e.g. when stories about the monster first appeared, famous sightings and what the monster might look like.
- Split the class into small groups and ask each one to research a mythological beast, e.g. Bigfoot, elves, vampires, werewolves. Pupils should create a short presentation, trying to persuade the government to fund a research mission to find their chosen beast.
- Ask pupils to locate Loch Ness on a map. As a class, make a list of some other famous places in Scotland, e.g. Glasgow, Edinburgh, Inverness, Glencoe. Give each pupil a blank map of Scotland and get them to label these places on their map. Pupils could use the Internet, atlases or road maps to help them.

Inverness
Loch Ness
Glencoe
Edinburgh
Glasgow

GRRRR

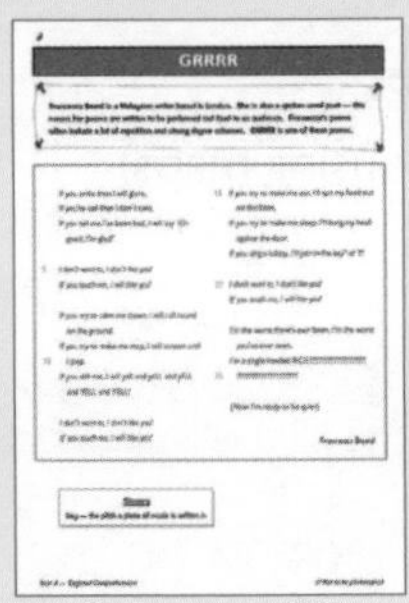

Question Book:
Year 4, pages 8-9

Author / Source:
Francesca Beard

Genre:
Poetry

Cross-curricular links:
- Drama (performance)

Introduction

This poem was written by the performance poet Francesca Beard. It is written from the perspective of a child who is having a tantrum. The unreasonable threats made by the narrator, as well as Beard's strong rhyme scheme, make the poem enjoyable to read. Beard uses a variety of punctuation and capitalisation to give directions on how her poem should be performed. As pupils read through the poem, encourage them to pick out any words that they think should be read in a particular way.

Answers

1. E.g. Because 'GRRRR' is an angry noise and the person speaking in the poem sounds angry.
2. glare and care; bad and glad
3. E.g. To show that the word should be read more loudly each time.
4. E.g. To show how angry the narrator is.
5. E.g. To make the last line seem calm and quiet.
6. E.g. I think a young child is talking, because the narrator is having a tantrum, and children often have tantrums. The narrator also mentions being fed and being sung a lullaby, which are things that parents often do for their children.
7. Any appropriate answer. E.g. No. I think the narrator sounds like trouble because they always want to do the opposite of what they're asked. They also sound very loud. OR E.g. Yes, because I think the narrator sounds funny. I'd like to see whether they would do all the things that they threaten to do.

Extra Activities

- Check pupils' understanding of the poem and ask whether they like it or not. As a class, discuss how the narrator feels at different points in the poem. Does their mood change at all?
- Explain to the class that onomatopoeia is when a word sounds like the type of noise it's describing. See if pupils can spot any examples of onomatopoeia in the poem, e.g. "pop", "shh" and "bang". Ask pupils to come up with their own examples then get them to present them on a poster with illustrations.
- Explain what a syllable is, and ask pupils to re-read the poem by themselves. How many syllables are in most of the words? As a class, discuss how this affects the rhythm of the poem.
- Ask pupils to make up their own poem, using the sentence structure that Beard uses throughout her poem ("If you... I will... "). E.g. "If you call me horrid names, I won't let you play my games". Encourage them to keep the mood of the poem lighthearted and tell them that it doesn't have to rhyme.
- Split the class into small groups and ask each group to prepare a performance of *GRRRR*. Remind pupils to think about the narrator's emotions in each line and how words written in capital letters or italics might need to be performed differently. Encourage them to be creative and add actions if they wish.

Julius Caesar's Goat

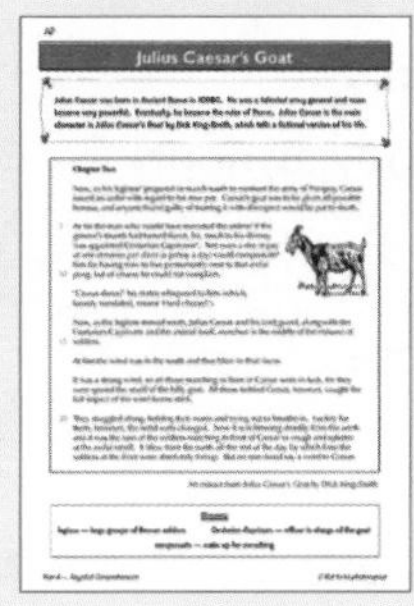

Question Book:
Year 4, pages 10-11

Author / Source:
Dick King-Smith

Genre:
Fiction — novel extract

Cross-curricular links:
- History (Ancient Rome)

Introduction

Julius Caesar's Goat is a lighthearted children's novel written by Dick King-Smith. Although most of the characters are historical (e.g. Julius Caesar and Cleopatra), the novel itself is a fictional account of Caesar's life in Ancient Rome. In this version of events, Caesar is accompanied by his faithful sidekick, Butter the goat. Butter gives off such a horrible smell that no one can bear to be around him, but Caesar doesn't realise because he has no sense of smell. Explain to pupils that Pompey was a rival of Caesar's and that, in this extract, Caesar and his men are marching to confront Pompey's army.

Answers

1. E.g. Because it smells really horrible.
2. E.g. I think the general had to make a decision about whether to kill the goat, and decided not to.
3. E.g. Unhappy. Even though he's getting paid more, it doesn't make up for the fact that he has to stay close to the smelly goat all the time.
4. E.g. tough luck!; hard luck!; too bad!
5. pong, stink
6. E.g. Because Caesar had ordered everyone to honour his goat. He threatened to kill anyone who didn't treat it with respect.
7. E.g. No, because the text is silly and makes fun of the Roman soldiers and Caesar. A story about a smelly goat is funny.

Extra Activities

- As a class, discuss pupils' answers to question 7 in the Question Book and explore what gives the extract its lighthearted tone, e.g. informal language, the character of the goat, the way the soldiers act.
- Show pupils a short extract from a non-fiction text about Julius Caesar. Ask pupils to identify the main differences between the way the non-fiction text is written compared to the extract by Dick King-Smith. Why do they think the two texts are different? Which text do they prefer and why?
- Explain that Caesar attempted to invade Britain twice, in 55 and 54BC. Get pupils to research Caesar's attempted invasions and then write a newspaper report from the perspective of the British army. They could include how Caesar attacked and how the British fought back.
- Ask pupils to research evidence of Roman remains near to their home town, e.g. Hadrian's Wall in the North, Chester's Roman amphitheatre, the Roman Baths in Bath. Get pupils to write a presentation about their chosen remains, designed to be read out in an assembly. It should be clear and informative.
- Split the class into groups and ask them to research the Roman army, e.g. what weaponry they used and what armour they wore. Get each group to draw and label a picture of a Roman soldier.

Armoured Dinosaurs

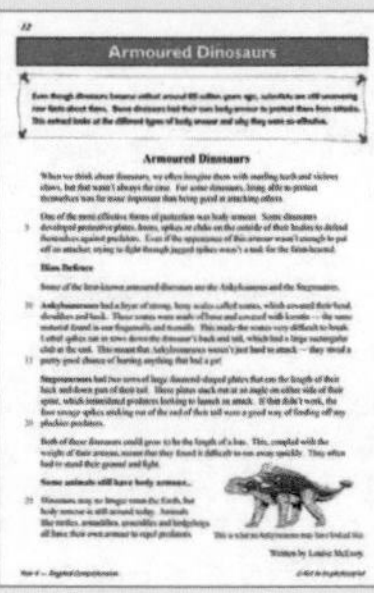

Question Book:
Year 4, pages 12-13

Author / Source:
Louise McEvoy

Genre:
Non-fiction — reference text

Cross-curricular links:
- Science (dinosaurs; body armour)
- Art (illustration)
- D&T (designing a dinosaur)

Introduction

This non-fiction extract focuses on dinosaurs with body armour, and how they protected themselves from predators. The text uses some presentational features which are commonly found in non-fiction texts. Before reading the text with the class, ask pupils if they've heard of the two dinosaurs named in the extract (Ankylosaurus and Stegosaurus). Do they know anything about them?

Answers

1. E.g. Because the "jagged spikes" would have made it difficult and dangerous for a predator to attack.
2. E.g. To make them stand out because they are key words.
3. Any two from: both had spikes; both had body armour on their backs; both had weapons at the end of their tails.
4. E.g. put off; scared; disheartened
5. b. Because they were very heavy.
6. E.g. A non-fiction text, because it gives the reader facts and information about a real-life topic.
7. E.g. Yes, because the text is divided into different sections using subheadings, so it's easy to find information. The picture of the Ankylosaurus helps you to understand what it might have looked like.

Extra Activities

- The text uses lots of adjectives. Ask pupils why they think the author might have done this. As a class, underline all the adjectives in the second paragraph (e.g. "effective", "protective", "jagged"), then get pupils to underline some adjectives in the rest of the text independently.
- Get pupils to research and write a similar extract on a different topic, e.g. dinosaurs that could fly, or dinosaurs that were herbivores. Pupils' pages should follow a similar structure to the extract (e.g. an introduction, detailed examples and a conclusion which links to modern animals) and contain some presentational features of non-fiction texts (e.g. images, headings, captions).
- Assign each pupil an extinct animal species, e.g. dodo, sabre-toothed cat, baiji white dolphin. Get them to find a picture of the animal and write a description of it using lots of their own adjectives. Then split the class into pairs and get pupils to swap their descriptions with their partner. Each pupil should try to draw their partner's animal based on the description they've been given.
- Ask pupils to research other animals that use body armour, e.g. turtles, hedgehogs, armadillos. Get them to produce a poster describing the animals' armour and explaining why it is effective against predators.
- Show the class pictures of various dinosaurs and discuss how they are adapted to their environment. Ask pupils to design their own dinosaur and draw an annotated picture of it. They should think about features the dinosaur will need to help it survive, e.g. body armour to protect itself from predators.

The Story of Nu Wa

Question Book:
Year 4, pages 14-15

Author / Source:
Holly Robinson

Genre:
Myth

Cross-curricular links:
- PSHE (myths across cultures)
- Science (the Earth's structure)
- Art (cartoon strip)

Introduction

The Story of Nu Wa is a myth that originated in China and was first recorded many centuries ago. The myth tells the story of how a goddess called Nu Wa saved the world from destruction after two warring gods split the sky and cracked open the Earth. Before pupils read the text, explain to them that different countries and cultures have their own myths and legends.

Answers

1. b. weaknesses
2. crowed. E.g. Because it means 'boasted' and Gong Gong is boasting about how powerful he is.
3. E.g. Because its summit is holding up the sky.
4. Any two from: the main characters are supernatural; it is set a very long time ago; the events of the story are supernatural; it is a story about gods and goddesses.
5. Any appropriate answer. E.g. Yes, because she mended the sky and crushed a dragon with her fingers.
6. E.g. No, they destroy the Earth with their selfishness. Gods are meant to protect the Earth. OR E.g. Yes, you would expect gods to be powerful, and Gong Gong is powerful enough to cause floods and to cause the sky to fall down.

Extra Activities

- As a class, discuss pupils' answers to question 4 in the Question Book and make a list of common features of myths. Ask pupils to write a recipe giving instructions on how to make a myth. Give examples to get them started, e.g. take a dollop of bravery and add a sprinkle of the supernatural.
- Tell pupils that myths were often used to explain natural phenomena. Ask pupils what phenomena this myth might be trying to explain (e.g. flooding and forest fires; how the sky is suspended above Earth). Ask pupils to research another myth, e.g. Pangu the Giant. Does it have any similarities to the myth of Nu Wa? Why do they think people all over the world tell these kinds of stories? Are myths still important in the modern world?
- As a class, discuss the Earth's structure (e.g. the crust, the mantle, the inner and outer cores) and get pupils to draw a labelled diagram of it. Pupils should then write their own myth about how the Earth came into being using the conventions of myths discussed in the first activity.
- Get pupils to create a cartoon strip telling the story of Nu Wa. Pupils should pay attention to how they think Nu Wa might have felt at different points in the story.

Coram Boy

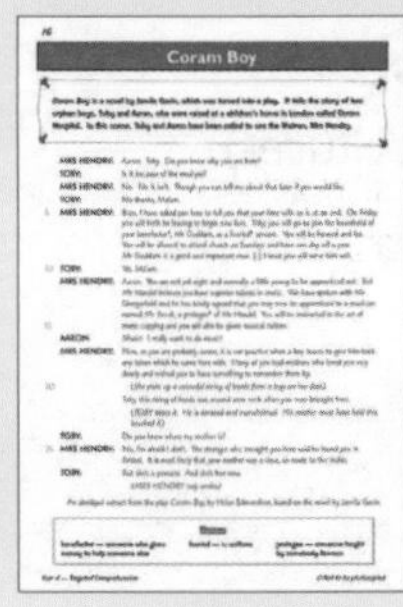

Question Book:
Year 4, pages 16-17

Author / Source:
Helen Edmundson (based on the novel by Jamila Gavin)

Genre:
Fiction — playscript

Cross-curricular links:
- Drama (performance)
- Music (classical music)

Introduction

Coram Boy is a novel by Jamila Gavin, which was first published in 2000. It won the Whitbread Children's Book Award and was made into a play in 2005. Set in 18th-century England, it follows the story of Toby, who was rescued from an African slave ship, and Aaron, the illegitimate son of a rich heir, who both live at Coram Hospital, a children's home. Explain to pupils that prior to the mid-1700s, children in London who were abandoned due to poverty or the death of a family member were often left to fend for themselves. Thomas Coram founded one of the first children's homes which looked after these abandoned children.

Answers

1. E.g. The stage directions in brackets and the characters' names written on the left.
2. E.g. He is worried, because he thinks that he is going to be told off for something to do with the mud pie.
3. E.g. Because the beads belonged to his mother, who he never knew.
4. E.g. She knows that his mother isn't a princess and she probably isn't free. She smiles because she's pretending to believe Toby.
5. Any appropriate answer. E.g. He might feel grateful because he's going to work for a man who has been supporting him and he's going to be given food and a place to stay. But he might also not be looking forward to it very much because he only gets one day off a year.

Extra Activities

- Building on pupils' responses to question 5, assign each child in the class the character of either Toby or Aaron. Get them to write a diary entry describing their feelings about leaving Coram Hospital. Ask them to discuss their diary entry with another pupil who wrote about a different character.
- Discuss with the class how playscripts try to mimic real speech to make the dialogue sound realistic. Ask pupils how Edmundson does this in the extract, e.g. one word sentences, sentences starting with "and".
- Ask pupils to write a script for another scene in the play, e.g. Toby's arrival at Mr Gaddarn's, Aaron's journey to meet Mr Brook. Pupils should use similar layout and written techniques to the extract.
- In the extract, Toby becomes emotional when he is handed the string of beads. Ask the pupils to think about an object that means a lot to them, e.g. a souvenir from holiday or a gift from someone close to them. Get them to write down what the object means to them and how it makes them feel. Invite pupils to share what they've written with the class.
- Split the class into groups and ask them to act out the extract. Encourage them to think about conveying the emotions of Toby and Aaron as Mrs Hendry tells them what is going to happen to them.
- Explain to the class that the "Mr Handel" mentioned in the extract was a famous composer. Play pupils an excerpt from Handel's 'Music for the Royal Fireworks'. How does it make them feel? Do they recognise any instruments? Without knowing the title, can they guess what occasion the music was composed for?

An Interview with Tim Peake

Question Book:
Year 4, pages 18-19

Author / Source:
www.destinationspace.uk

Genre:
Non-fiction — interview

Cross-curricular links:
- D&T (designing a patch)
- Science (gravity)

Introduction

Tim Peake was interested in flying from a young age. In 1992, he graduated from Sandhurst as a British Army officer and went on to work as an army pilot, flying instructor and test pilot. In 2008, he applied to become an astronaut with the European Space Agency (ESA). Out of more than 8000 applicants, he was one of six to be selected. In December 2015, he became the first British man to live on the International Space Station (ISS), spending 185 days in space. Tim gave this interview shortly before he travelled to the ISS.

Answers

1. Going on a spacewalk.
2. E.g. The space station doesn't have night and day like Earth does. This would make it difficult to sleep because you usually go to sleep when it's dark, but sometimes it wouldn't be dark at bedtime.
3. E.g. Astronauts have important and sometimes dangerous jobs to do on the Space Station, for example spacewalks, so keeping calm in difficult situations will help them do their job better.
4. E.g. very important; essential; vital
5. E.g. The questions are written in bold and separated from the answers. This makes them easy to spot.
6. Any appropriate answer. E.g. It is different because you can't just go outside like you would on Earth. However, it's also similar because you can do things like watching TV and playing the guitar.
7. Any appropriate answer. E.g. Yes. It would be interesting to see the Earth from space and I would feel proud because going into space is something that very few people get the chance to do. OR E.g. No. I would be scared to go into space because it's so far from home and something might go wrong.

Extra Activities

- Get pupils to imagine that they are in a rocket that is about to launch. Ask them to write a few paragraphs describing how they feel about going into space.
- Ask pupils to produce a short biography about Tim. They could write about his early life, his journey to becoming an astronaut, the work of the International Space Station and what Tim achieved in the six months he was up there.
- Get pupils to think of a question they would like to ask Tim about space and his time on the International Space Station. Pupils should ask their question to a partner, who should answer in character as Tim.
- Split the class into groups. Get each group to research a different aspect of life for astronauts in space, e.g. what they eat, how they sleep, how they exercise. Each group should present their findings to the class.
- Explain that Blue Peter held a competition to design a patch that Tim would wear on his space suit. Get pupils to design their own patch that reflects the mission and its aims.
- Ask the class what they know about how gravity works on Earth, then show them a video from the ISS demonstrating zero gravity. Discuss with pupils how and why gravity is different in space than on Earth.

Escape From Germany

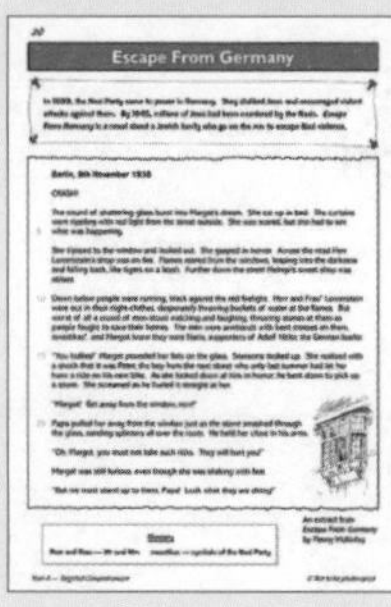

Question Book:
Year 4, pages 20-21

Author / Source:
Penny McKinlay

Genre:
Fiction — novel extract

Cross-curricular links:
- History (Nazi Germany)
- PSHE (prejudice)

Introduction

Escape from Germany by Penny McKinlay is part of the *Sparks* series, a range of books that introduce children to historical events and the experiences of people who lived through them. Explain to the class that this extract takes place during Kristallnacht or the 'Night of Broken Glass', a Nazi attack on Jews that took place on the night of 9-10 November 1938. Jews throughout Germany were attacked and their schools, homes, businesses and synagogues were vandalised or burnt. You may want to show pupils some photos that show the extent of the devastation.

Answers

1. E.g. Because some shops on her street are on fire.
2. E.g. To help you imagine how the flames are leaping like a tiger wanting to attack, then disappearing as if they are being tugged back on a lead.
3. E.g. To get away from the fire.
4. a. It is in capitals. b. E.g. To grab the reader's attention and show how sudden and loud the noise was.
5. E.g. She might feel angry and betrayed. He was nice to her when he let her ride on his new bike, but now he is joining in with the violence by throwing a stone at her.
6. Any appropriate answer. E.g. It tells you that she's brave because she stands up to the people outside. She calls them "bullies" and doesn't want to just hide away from them.

Extra Activities

- Get pupils to write a letter from Peter to Margot giving his version of the events in the extract. Pupils could consider how Peter was feeling, why he might have thrown the stone and if he feels sorry or not.
- Ask pupils to share their answers to question 2 in the Question Book and discuss the effect of the simile "like tigers on a leash". Make sure pupils understand what a simile is and ask them to create their own similes to describe fire. They could use some of their examples to write a poem about fire.
- As a class, discuss pupils' answers to question 4b in the Question Book. Is this an effective way to start a story? Ask them to suggest other opening words that would have a similar impact. Then ask pupils to choose one of the words they have suggested and use it as the opening line for their own short story.
- Ask pupils to write a newspaper article reporting the events described in the extract. Remind them about the layout features of newspaper articles including headlines, subheadings and columns.
- Explain to pupils a little about how the Nazi Party treated the Jews whilst it was in power and ask pupils to put themselves in Margot's shoes. How would they feel and what would they do? Discuss what they think about the actions of people such as Peter, the boy who throws a stone at Margot in the extract. Why do they think some people in Germany behaved in this way?

Poems about the Weather

Question Book:
Year 4, pages 22-23

Author / Source:
Robert Louis Stevenson
Carol Ann Duffy

Genre:
Poetry

Cross-curricular links:
- Art (illustration)
- Music (mood)

Introduction

Scottish writer Robert Louis Stevenson (1850-1894) published numerous children's poems. His creative use of language and imagery to describe familiar experiences gave his poems a lasting appeal, and many are still included in children's poetry anthologies to this day. Carol Ann Duffy became the UK's Poet Laureate in 2009 and has composed poems for many important national events. She is known for her use of simple language to create powerful, striking images. Despite being written more than 100 years apart, these two poems offer clear points of comparison in terms of their subject matter, narrative point of view and poetic techniques.

Answers

1. *The Wind*
2. E.g. throw; fling; hurl
3. Any appropriate answer. E.g. Invisible. The narrator says that he can feel and hear the wind and see the things it does, but he can't see the wind itself.
4. E.g. raindrops
5. E.g. Thunderstorms, because the narrator says "I love your thunderstorm dress" but only says "I like" for the other dresses.
6. d. a verb
7. Any appropriate answer. E.g. I prefer *The Wind* because I like the idea of the wind as an invisible creature, singing and throwing things around. OR E.g. I prefer *Your Dresses* because I like the way that the descriptions of the dresses sound like different types of weather.

Extra Activities

- As a class, discuss similarities and differences in the form and structure of the two poems, then create a table comparing them. The table could include things like number of stanzas, number of lines in each stanza, rhyming pattern and use of repetition.
- Both poems use personification to bring the weather to life. Remind pupils what personification is, then encourage them to pick out some examples from the poems (e.g. "I heard you call", "when you dance on the lawn"). As a class, discuss why poets use personification and its effect on the reader. Ask them to choose one example of personification from either of the poems and create an illustration of it.
- As a class, discuss the different seasons. Which one do pupils prefer, and why? Ask pupils to write their own poem with a verse for each season. They should start each verse in a similar style to Duffy, e.g. "I like (summer)", and use "But I love (autumn)" to introduce their favourite one.
- These poems look at how weather can create different moods. Explain that the composer Vivaldi wrote a group of concertos called *The Four Seasons*. Each concerto represents the season it's named after. Play pupils an excerpt from one of the concertos (either spring, summer, autumn or winter) and ask them to use the mood of the piece to guess which season they think the music represents.

Wayne Rooney: Captain of England

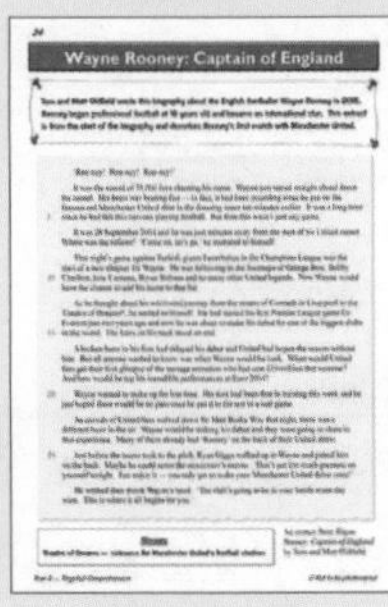

Question Book:
Year 4, pages 24-25

Author / Source:
Tom and Matt Oldfield

Genre:
Non-fiction — biography

Cross-curricular links:

- PE (football)
- Maths (measurement)

Introduction

Wayne Rooney was born in Croxteth, Liverpool in 1985. He is regarded by some as the best footballer in England and one of the best in the world. He showed promise from a very young age, joining the Everton Academy aged 9 and making his professional debut for the club at 16. He made his first appearance for England aged 17 and his talent was soon recognised by Manchester United, who bought the striker for £25.6 million when he was 18. He is one of Manchester United and England's top goalscorers. Before pupils read the extract, ask them if they support any football teams.

Answers

1. E.g. To show that the words are being chanted by the crowd.
2. E.g. Because it was his first game playing for Manchester United, so it was very important to him.
3. a. an adjective
   b. E.g. Whirlwinds move very fast, so it suggests that Rooney's career has moved quickly.
4. E.g. first appearance; introduction; entrance
5. E.g. Because he had a broken bone in his foot.
6. E.g. They are excited to see Rooney play for their club for the first time. There is a "buzz" in the air and many of them have his name on their shirts.
7. Any appropriate answer. E.g. Because it was a very significant moment in his life. As it says in the last line, this match was where his career really began.

Extra Activities

- Ask pupils to write a diary entry from Rooney's perspective on the night before his Manchester United debut. They should use information from the extract to help them imagine how he might be feeling.
- As a class, make a list of the features of biographies, then ask pupils if they can identify any of them in the extract. Invite pupils to research a sportsperson they admire and write a short biography about them.
- Divide pupils into small groups and ask each group to create a football-based activity to be used in a PE lesson. Pupils should write instructions for their activity, explaining how it works and what equipment they'll need. Each group should present their idea to the class, who will then vote for their favourite activity. The winning activity could be used in their next PE lesson.
- Wayne Rooney is known for his goal-scoring ability. Have a PE lesson with the class on dribbling and striking. Set up a goal and arrange a line of cones in front of it. Get pupils to dribble the ball in and out of all of the cones, before striking the ball into the net (there doesn't need to be a goalkeeper).
- Give pupils the dimensions of a standard football pitch and ask them to work out its perimeter. Repeat this exercise with other playing fields, e.g. tennis, netball, rugby.

The Lion, the Witch and the Wardrobe

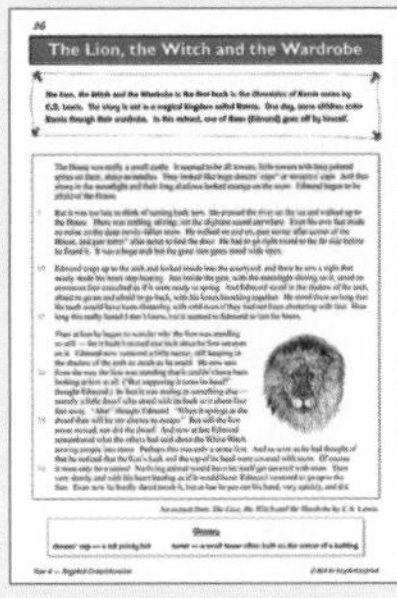

Question Book:
Year 4, pages 26-27

Author / Source:
C.S. Lewis

Genre:
Classic fiction — novel extract

Cross-curricular links:
- Art (illustration)
- Science (lions)
- D&T (clay models)

Introduction

C.S. Lewis is best known for his seven-part fantasy series, *The Chronicles of Narnia. The Lion, the Witch and the Wardrobe* is the first book in the series. It focuses on four siblings, Peter, Susan, Edmund and Lucy, who help to free the magical kingdom of Narnia from the power of the evil White Witch. In this extract, Edmund, who has been corrupted by the White Witch, has snuck away from his siblings to visit the Witch's castle. Before reading the extract, ask pupils if they are familiar with the Narnia books or films.

Answers

1. E.g. No, because sharp things like "needles" might hurt you, so this description makes the house sound threatening and dangerous.
2. E.g. Each word is repeated. The author did this to show how big the house is and how far Edmund had to walk to find the entrance.
3. a. a verb
4. E.g. It is winter — there is deep snow on the ground and the river has frozen over.
5. E.g. To show how scared and nervous Edmund is. It helps you to put yourself in Edmund's place and imagine exactly how he feels.
6. Any appropriate answer. E.g. No. Edmund has heard that the White Witch can turn people into stone. This makes her sound frightening and dangerous, so I would be scared to meet her.

Extra Activities

- The extract ends with Edmund putting out his hand to touch the lion. Get each pupil to write a few bullet points summarising what they think might happen next. Each pupil should swap their summary with a partner and then write a continuation of the story based on their partner's summary.
- As a class, discuss how the author shows that Edmund is scared in the third paragraph. Do pupils think that the author's techniques are effective? Assign pupils other emotions (e.g. happy, sad, angry) and get them to write a paragraph using similar techniques to describe how they feel.
- Invite pupils to make up their own magical land like Narnia. What would they call it? What would its inhabitants be like? How would you travel to this world? Ask pupils to write a short story about a group of children discovering their magical land.
- Using information from the text and their own imaginations, ask pupils to draw the Witch's castle. Encourage them to include as much detail as possible and to try to capture the atmosphere of the extract.
- Ask pupils to produce a fact sheet about lions. They should include information about where lions live and their diet, as well as illustrations. The sheets could then be made into a class display.
- Get pupils to make a model lion from clay. They should use their fact sheets from the previous activity to make their models as accurate as possible.

A Letter from Barack Obama

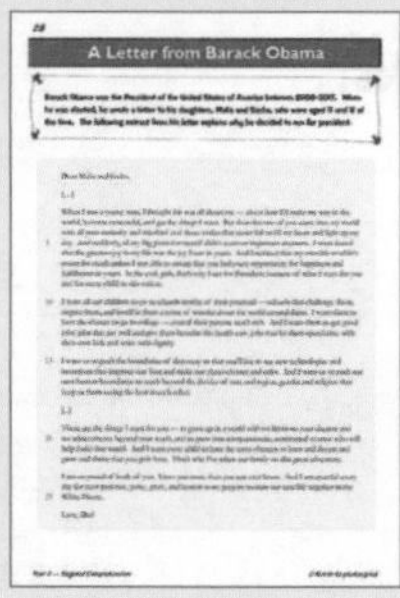

Question Book:
Year 4, pages 28-29

Author / Source:
Barack Obama

Genre:
Non-fiction — letter

Cross-curricular links:
- PSHE (social responsibility)

Introduction

Barack Obama was elected in November 2008 and sworn in as President of the United States in January 2009. Born in Honolulu, Hawaii, Obama trained and worked as a lawyer before entering politics. In this letter to his daughters, he explains his reasons for running for President and what he hoped to achieve during his time in office. Before pupils read the letter, ask them what they know about Obama. Have they seen him on television or heard his speeches? What is their opinion of him?

Answers

1. E.g. He became less selfish.
2. E.g. That children should go to schools that will help them achieve their very best.
3. E.g. Yes, he says good jobs pay well, which means people will have the money to buy things they need. He also says that good jobs give people benefits like healthcare, so having a good job helps people to look after their health.
4. E.g. Differences caused by race, region, gender and religion.
5. E.g. Barack becoming the President and his family moving to the White House.
6. E.g. He is caring because he wants to help people go to good schools and get good jobs. He is ambitious because he tells his daughters the things he wants to do to help make the world a better place.
7. Any appropriate answer. E.g. It might be hard because they would be busy and I might not get to see them very much. It might also be exciting because the President and his family probably travel a lot, so I might get to visit new countries.

Extra Activities

- Explain that politicians often write and talk in a persuasive way. Discuss with the class some of the persuasive features of the letter, e.g. lists of three, emotive adjectives, personal pronouns.
- Ask pupils to think about the different features of letter writing, e.g. its layout, the type of language used. Drawing on this discussion, ask them to write a letter to Obama from the perspective of one of his children. Encourage pupils to write about their hopes and fears about their father becoming President.
- Explain to pupils that a magazine asked Obama to write this letter so that they could publish it. How might publishing this letter in a magazine change the intended audience?
- Split the class into groups. Ask each group to think of ways to improve issues affecting their school, e.g. littering, after school clubs, school dinners. Pupils should write their ideas in a table, which has columns for the 'pros' and 'cons' of each suggestion. Hold a mock election where each group puts forward their solutions. Pupils can then vote for the most convincing group.
- Discuss how Obama wants to make a difference in the world. Get pupils to think about something they could do, however small, to make a difference in their community e.g. picking up a piece of litter and putting it in the bin. Give pupils a week to perform a good deed, then as a class discuss what they did.

The Jungle Book

Question Book:
Year 4, pages 30-31

Author / Source:
Rudyard Kipling

Genre:
Classic fiction — novel extract

Cross-curricular links:
- Geography (India)
- Drama (miming)
- PSHE (differences)

Introduction

The Jungle Book, Kipling's collection of stories about Mowgli, is often considered a children's classic. It is one of Kipling's best-known works and was influenced by his experiences of living in India, the country of his birth. Kipling moved to England at the age of 5, but later returned to India to work as a journalist. Before reading the extract with the class, ask pupils if they are familiar with the story or adaptations of it, such as the popular 1967 Disney® film or the 2016 live-action remake.

Answers

1. E.g. He was involved in a fight and made a "bad enemy", so he fled from the jungle to get away from them.
2. E.g. Scared and threatened because they call out and run away from him. Mowgli is a stranger and probably looks very different to them, so they might think he's dangerous.
3. E.g. obstacle; barrier; fence
4. E.g. He can't use language to speak to the man, so he uses actions that he thinks the man will understand.
5. E.g. At first the villagers are frightened and alarmed by Mowgli, but when they realise he is just a child who has been living with wolves, they become more understanding and feel sorry for him.
6. Any appropriate answer. E.g. Yes. I want to read more about Mowgli and find out if he was the boy who was taken by the tiger. I also want to know more about the fight at Council Rock.

Extra Activities

- Ask pupils to write a diary entry from the perspective of one of the villagers recounting Mowgli's arrival.
- As a class, discuss what evidence Kipling gives that the villagers are afraid of the jungle and why they might be so afraid. Get pupils to write a short story explaining why the villagers are so afraid.
- Discuss with pupils why Mowgli may have been forced to leave the jungle. Ask them to write a couple of paragraphs describing what happened. Then get them to swap and discuss their work with a partner.
- With the class, find India on a map of the world. Get pupils to draw and label India, and the countries and seas that surround it. They should also label the main geographical features and regions of India, e.g. Himalayan mountain range, River Ganges, rainforest, main cities.
- In the extract, Mowgli has to ask a villager for food by using actions. Split the class into pairs and get each pupil to see if they can successfully ask their partner something without using words.
- Explain that later on in the novel, Mowgli is driven out of the village because the villagers are afraid of his ability to communicate with animals. Discuss the difficulties they think Mowgli would have in trying to fit in with the wolves in the pack and the humans in the village. Do pupils think it was right of the villagers to turn Mowgli away because they were scared of him?

Gertrude Ederle

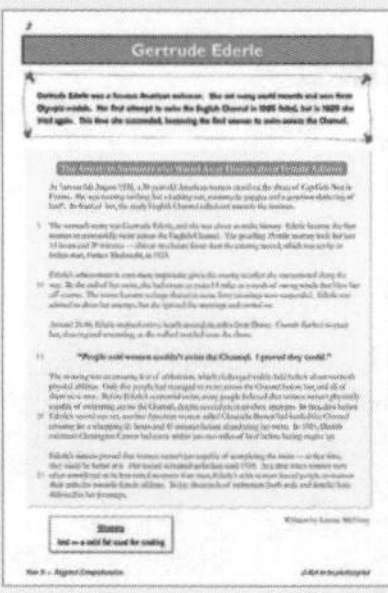
Gertrude Ederle

Question Book:
Year 5, pages 2-3

Author / Source:
Louise McEvoy

Genre:
Non-fiction — article

Cross-curricular links:

- PSHE (gender equality)
- PE (water safety; circuit training)

Introduction

Gertrude Ederle is best known for being the first woman to swim the English Channel. Her achievement was greatly celebrated, and she became an American superstar. Ederle went on to play herself in a Hollywood movie and gave swimming demonstrations across the USA. This article documents Ederle's 1926 Channel swim and describes how it changed the way people viewed women's sport. Before pupils read the article, discuss what they think attitudes towards women were like in the 1920s. How were they different to attitudes today?

Answers

1. E.g. Because the article is about swimming in the sea, so "waved away" is a play on words. It means 'dismisses', but it could also be talking about the waves on the sea.
2. E.g. "Steely" makes the sea sound uninviting. It suggests that the sea is grey and makes it sound cold.
3. E.g. Because it's a quote from Gertrude, so it's an important part of the text. It also introduces the next section of the article.
4. E.g. achievement; accomplishment; act
5. E.g. It made people think women could be just as good at sport as men because it proved that a woman could break a sporting record set by a man.
6. Any appropriate answer. E.g. She was brave because she carried on swimming even though she was advised to stop. She was also determined because she swam the Channel, even though some women had failed before she made her attempt.

Extra Activities

- Explain that New York City held a celebratory parade for Gertrude when she returned home. Ask pupils to write a diary entry from Gertrude's perspective the day after the parade. Encourage pupils to imagine Gertrude's experiences during the parade and her feelings about her achievement.
- Ask pupils to imagine that the school wants to organise a visit from a famous sportsperson. Get pupils to think of a sportsman or sportswoman they would like to invite, then research their main achievements. Pupils should use their findings to write a short speech persuading the school to consider their choice. They should explain why their sportsperson is a good role model and how they inspire others.
- Give pupils two minutes to list as many sportspeople as they can, then ask them to count the number of men and women on their lists. Are they surprised by the results? As a class, discuss why sportsmen are generally more famous than sportswomen. Do pupils think this will ever change?
- Ask pupils to research safety tips for swimming in the sea, then get them to create a leaflet about water safety. Pupils should include useful 'dos' and 'don'ts', and advice on what to do if you get into difficulty.
- Explain that circuit training is a good way to build fitness for sports like swimming. Get pupils to write simple instructions for activities you could use in circuit training (e.g. sit-ups, star jumps). Use ten of the activities for a PE lesson. Pupils should do each activity for one minute, with 30 seconds' rest in between.

The Unluckiest Boy in the World

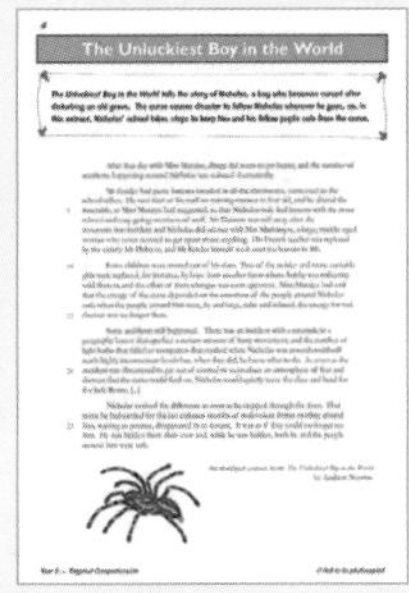

Question Book:
Year 5, pages 4-5

Author / Source:
Andrew Norriss

Genre:
Fiction — novel extract

Cross-curricular links:

- PSHE (loneliness)
- Art (cartoon strip)

Introduction

Andrew Norriss worked as a history teacher before becoming a full-time writer when he was in his mid-thirties. He has written several popular novels for young people, as well as a number of successful children's television series, including *Woof!* and *Bernard's Watch.* He is known for his light-hearted, comical writing style. After reading the introduction, ask pupils to share what they know about curses with the rest of the class. Ask if they have heard of any rumoured curses in real life, e.g. the curse of Tutankhamun.

Answers

1. E.g. The curse caused lots of strange accidents, like a mountain-lion getting into the school.
2. E.g. in general; normally; most of the time
3. third
4. E.g. evil; malicious; hostile
5. Any appropriate answer. E.g. Yes, because they've surrounded Nicholas with calm people, which reduces the strength of the curse. They've also made the Safe Room, which hides Nicholas from the curse. OR E.g. No, because the curse is supernatural, so I don't think it can be stopped by such simple changes. I think it will find a way to overcome the changes and keep on affecting Nicholas and those around him.
6. Any appropriate answer. E.g. He might feel angry and upset that the curse causes people to get hurt. He might also feel guilty that he's partly responsible for the bad things that happen.
7. Any appropriate answer. E.g. No, although the curse makes it difficult for him to lead a totally normal life, Nicholas can still go to school and he is surrounded by people who care about him. Some people face much worse situations than Nicholas. OR E.g. Yes, lots of bad things happen when he's around, like the "mountain-lion incident" and the "incident with a tarantula", so I think he is really unlucky.

Extra Activities

- Ask pupils to write a review of the extract, explaining what they did and didn't like about it.
- Make sure pupils understand the concept of comparatives and superlatives, then ask them to identify the superlative in the extract's title and some comparatives in the first three paragraphs of the extract (e.g. "better", "noisier", "more excitable"). Get pupils to write down ten more adjectives and form their comparatives and superlatives.
- Get pupils to come up with their own imaginary curse and ask them to write a short story about it.
- In *The Unluckiest Boy in the World*, the curse makes it difficult for Nicholas to make friends. In small groups, get pupils to discuss the issues of loneliness and isolation. Can they think of a time when they felt lonely? How does it feel to be alone? How can they prevent other pupils from feeling isolated or lonely?
- Ask pupils to imagine what they think happened during the "mountain-lion incident" mentioned in line 7 of the extract. Get them to draw a cartoon strip to tell the story.

Baby Birds

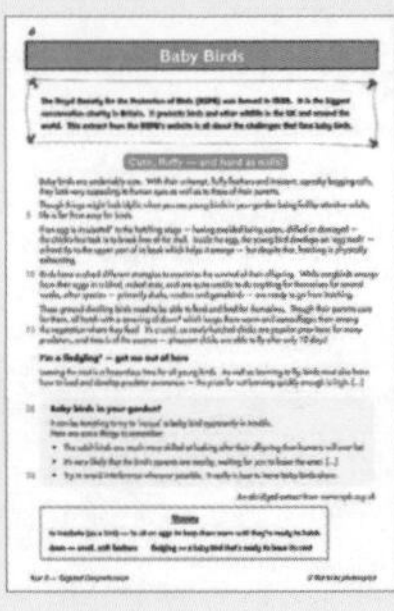

Question Book:
Year 5, pages 6-7

Author / Source:
www.rspb.org.uk

Genre:
Non-fiction — information text

Cross-curricular links:

- Science (garden birds)
- Maths (statistics)

Introduction

The RSPB was founded in 1889 to campaign against the killing of birds in order to use their plumages in clothing. Since then, it has grown into the UK's largest nature conservation charity, with over a million members and 200 nature reserves. The charity aims to protect the natural world, and it runs conservation projects in Britain and around the world. Before pupils read the text, get them to write down five adjectives that they would use to describe baby birds.

Answers

1. E.g. They aren't just cute — they're also quite tough.
2. d. alliteration
3. E.g. Because they don't have any feathers, so it's hard for them to keep warm. Also, they can't see, so they rely on their parents to do everything for them.
4. E.g. dangerous; risky; perilous
5. E.g. Because they're subheadings, so they need to stand out from the rest of the text.
6. E.g. Not getting enough to eat or being caught by a predator.
7. E.g. To separate the points about what to do if you find a baby bird and to make them stand out, so it's easier for the reader to remember them.
8. Any appropriate answer. E.g. To help protect birds by informing people about what they should do if they find a baby bird in their garden.

Extra Activities

- As a class, discuss the words that pupils wrote down before reading the article. Has the article changed their view of baby birds at all? Would they use any different words to describe baby birds now?
- Show pupils photos of some birds (e.g. a duckling, a sparrowhawk) and ask them to suggest alliterative phrases to describe them. Pupils could use their phrases to write a poem describing one of the birds.
- Get pupils to write and illustrate a story about a baby bird. They should use the information in the extract and their own imaginations to describe the bird's experiences as it hatches and develops.
- Assign pupils common garden birds (e.g. robins, sparrows, blue tits). Pupils should research their bird and design an informative poster that describes its appearance, calls, behaviour and habitat.
- Ask pupils to keep a tally of the different birds they see outside their home or in the school grounds. To help them identify the birds, pupils could use the posters from the previous activity or the Internet. Using a computer, pupils should then create a pictogram to display their results. As a class, collate all the pupils' results. How many different types of bird were seen? Which bird was most common?
- Split the class into groups and get them to research the RSPB, e.g. its history, its aims, and some of the work that the charity does. Then, as a class, discuss what pupils found out.

Johnny and the Dead

Johnny and the Dead

Question Book:
Year 5, pages 8-9

Author / Source:
Terry Pratchett
Stephen Briggs

Genre:
Fiction — playscript

Cross-curricular links:
- Drama (script-writing; performance)
- D&T (3D models)

Introduction

Terry Pratchett was a hugely popular fantasy novelist who was the UK's bestselling author of the 1990s. Pratchett's novel *Johnny and the Dead* was first published in 1993. In the novel, Johnny sees and talks to dead people in the cemetery near his home. When the local council plans to build on the graveyard, Johnny and the residents of the cemetery put together a plan to stop them. The story was turned into a play by Stephen Briggs in 1996. Before reading the extract with the class, ask pupils whether they have ever seen a stage or film adaptation of a book.

Answers

1. E.g. Because they tell you where the scene takes place and what it looks like.
2. E.g. To make it easy for actors to spot their lines when they act out the script.
3. E.g. To suggest that Wobbler's stammering because he's afraid.
4. E.g. Pretending to be a zombie.
5. E.g. He is scared by Johnny's behaviour, so he makes an excuse to leave. The stage directions say that he starts to run, which shows that he wants to get away from Johnny as quickly as he can.
6. E.g. Because Johnny is acting as a narrator as well as a character. This means Johnny can explain directly to the audience what is happening and how he is feeling.
7. Any appropriate answer. E.g. *The Bed and Breakfast Star* by Jacqueline Wilson because I really like the main character, Elsa, so I'd enjoy seeing her brought to life in a play. Also, I think the hotel room in the book would work well as a stage set.

Extra Activities

- Get pupils to write a diary entry from Johnny's perspective about the events of the script.
- Ask pupils to imagine they are standing in front of a door that has something frightening behind it. What would be behind the door? How would they feel? Would they knock on the door? Get them to write a short monologue describing their thoughts and feelings as they stand in front of the door.
- As a class, discuss whether pupils prefer to read books or watch their film adaptations. Ask them to justify their opinions.
- Ask pupils to choose a short extract from a novel they like and rewrite it in the form of a playscript. Make sure pupils use an appropriate layout and include clear stage directions in their scripts.
- Choose the most suitable playscripts and ask pupils to perform them. Encourage pupils to think about how they can convey their characters' emotions through their tone of voice, gestures and body language.
- Get pupils to design a set for the scene from *Johnny and the Dead*, or for the script they wrote for the fourth activity. They could sketch their design first, and then make a 3D model inside a shoebox.

Goodnight Mister Tom

Question Book:
Year 5, pages 10-11

Author / Source:
Michelle Magorian

Genre:
Fiction — novel extract

Cross-curricular links:
- Drama (role play)
- History (propaganda; WW2 rationing)
- Science (nutrition)

Introduction

Published in 1981, *Goodnight Mister Tom* was Michelle Magorian's first novel. It has proven so popular with audiences that it has been adapted for both stage and screen. The story begins just before the outbreak of the Second World War, when the protagonist, Willie, is evacuated from his abusive home in London and sent to live with an elderly widower called Mister Tom. Although Tom seems bad-tempered and unwelcoming at first, the pair form a close bond. Before pupils read the text, make sure they understand the concept of evacuation.

Answers

1. E.g. To help the reader imagine how Tom's accent sounds.
2. E.g. She feels uncomfortable. She gives Tom "an awkward smile" and blushes when she's talking to him.
3. E.g. confused; puzzled; perplexed
4. E.g. It makes the reader feel sorry for the girl. She is "tiny" and holds on to a "teddy-bear" which makes her sound very young and vulnerable.
5. Yes — he says that it's "obligatory".
6. Any appropriate answer. E.g. To make the story seem more realistic.
7. Any appropriate answer. E.g. No, because Tom seems very grumpy, so I think he will be unkind and impatient towards the boy. The boy sounds weak and unwell, so I think he will be frightened of Tom. OR E.g. Yes, because sometimes people who seem grumpy are actually kind underneath. I think Tom will feel sorry for the boy because he's "thin and sickly-looking" and so he'll take good care of him.

Extra Activities

- Split the class into groups of three and give the pupils in each group the roles of Tom, Willie and one of the other evacuees. Pupils should take turns to interview each other about how their characters' feelings change as the extract progresses. Encourage pupils to stay in character while they are being interviewed.
- Get pupils to rewrite the extract in the first person, from the perspective of the character they were assigned for the first activity. Pupils could then compare their work and discuss how and why the characters might see the same episode differently.
- Show pupils some examples of Second World War propaganda posters (e.g. from the National Archives) that encouraged people on the home front to contribute to the war effort. As a class, discuss the message of the posters — why were things like growing food and avoiding waste important during the war? Get pupils to explain the techniques used to make the posters persuasive, then challenge them to create their own wartime propaganda posters, using similar techniques.
- Direct pupils to a reliable source, e.g. the BBC Primary History website, and ask them to make a list of foods that were rationed in Britain during the Second World War. Were there any foods that were unavailable? As a class, discuss the similarities and differences between children's diets today and during the war. Would pupils enjoy eating war rations? Which diet do they think is healthier?

Facts about Hurricanes!

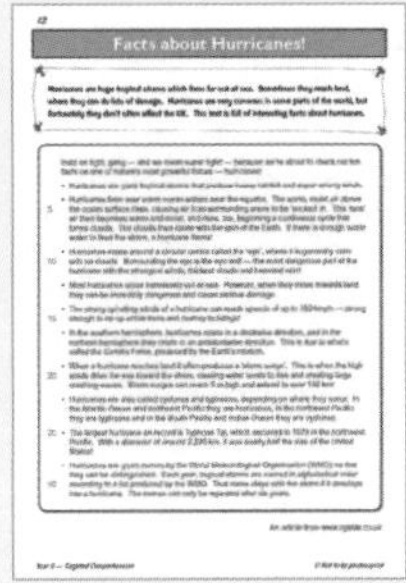

Question Book:
Year 5, pages 12-13

Author / Source:
www.ngkids.co.uk

Genre:
Non-fiction — reference text

Cross-curricular links:

- Geography (weather)
- Art (mood boards)

Introduction

Hurricanes are huge, rotating storms that form over tropical oceans. They can be more than 2000 km across, and can cause winds of over 300 kmph. They also bring heavy rain and powerful thunderstorms, and can cause serious flooding, particularly in coastal areas. Although Britain is too far north to be hit by tropical hurricanes, it is sometimes affected by major storm systems from the Atlantic, such as the Great Storm of 1987. Before pupils read the article, check their understanding of some key terms in the extract, e.g. diameter, equator, northern hemisphere and southern hemisphere.

Answers

1. E.g. To emphasise how strong the winds are during a hurricane.
2. E.g. Because they form from the warm, moist air that's found rising above the surface of warm oceans.
3. E.g. Younger people, because the introduction uses chatty language such as "super tight" and calls the readers "gang".
4. E.g. To show that lots of the facts about hurricanes are interesting and impressive.
5. E.g. To help you imagine how big the storm was by giving you something to compare it to.
6. b. to inform and entertain
7. E.g. Because they don't affect people too much at sea, but when they reach land they can cause dangerous floods, and the high winds can kill or injure people by knocking down buildings and trees.

Extra Activities

- With the whole class, discuss the layout of the text. Do pupils find the layout helpful? Can they think of any other layout features (e.g. subheadings, underlining, diagrams) that would make the text clearer and easier to read?
- Show pupils some pictures of the damage caused by the Great Storm of 1987, then ask them to research the storm. They should use their findings to produce a fact sheet about the storm and how it affected people. Encourage pupils to use the presentational devices discussed in the activity above, such as headings, subheadings and bullet points.
- Show the class some short videos of hurricanes. Ask pupils to come up with phrases that use figurative language (e.g. similes, metaphors, personification, onomatopoeia) to describe the weather conditions.
- Ask pupils to imagine what it would be like to experience a hurricane. Get them to write a letter to a friend describing the experience and how it made them feel.
- Assign pupils different types of weather (e.g. rain, snow, thunderstorms). Ask them to create a mood board showing the words, colours, activities and feelings they associate with that type of weather. As a class, compare the mood boards and discuss the similarities and differences between them.

Poems about Words

Question Book:
Year 5, pages 14-15

Author / Source:
Adisa
Maya Angelou

Genre:
Poetry

Cross-curricular links:
- Drama (performance)
- Art (illustrating imagery)

Introduction

As a performance poet, Adisa writes poems which are intended to be spoken aloud. His poetry uses language in a playful way, seeking to entertain the audience and make them think. Maya Angelou was a renowned American poet, writer and civil rights activist. Like Adisa, her poems are often lively and playful, with an element of performance to them. These poems both use vivid imagery, including images of food, to convey an enjoyment of language and words. You may want to ask pupils to read the poems aloud.

Answers

1. "they pop up and down / Like a Jamaican toaster"
2. E.g. It makes the reader feel more involved in the poem because it seems like the poet is talking directly to them.
3. a. E.g. The things you read have a big effect on you because they stay in your mind for a long time. The poet says this is a good thing — like the smell of buttered popcorn. b. E.g. The message is quite similar because it also says that reading can have a really big effect on you. However, it's a bit different, because it says, "Be afraid", which makes you think that the effects of reading might be dangerous.
4. Any appropriate answer. E.g. Because they both enjoy words so much that they crave them, in the same way that people crave their favourite foods. They also want to show that bodies absorb and process words, just like they eat and digest food.
5. Any appropriate answer. E.g. *Spellbound*, because lines like "On this lyrical roller coaster" make the poem seem fun and exciting. I also like the way the poet plays with words like "lip-hop" instead of "hip-hop". OR E.g. *I Love the Look of Words*, because I think the description of eating popcorn is very effective, and I think it is a really good idea to compare reading to eating something delicious.

Extra Activities

- With the whole class, discuss the form, rhyme scheme and rhythm of the two poems. Encourage pupils to identify similarities and differences between them.
- Get pupils to identify examples of word-play in *Spellbound* (e.g. "lip-hop", "tongue-tied like Houdini" — you may need to explain who Houdini was). Ask them to explain their meaning and effect on the reader, then challenge them to think of their own examples of word-play relating to the theme of reading.
- Ask pupils to write a poem about their favourite hobby. They should use imaginative imagery and word-play to explain what they like about their hobby.
- Get pupils to choose a verse from either poem, and ask them to learn it by heart and then recite it to the class. Encourage pupils to pay attention to their pace and tone of voice as they perform their verse.
- Split the class into four groups and ask each group to create an illustration based on the imagery in one stanza of *Spellbound*. Each group should then present their illustration to the class and explain how it relates to the poem.

The Oak and the Linden Tree

The Oak and the Linden Tree

Question Book:
Year 5, pages 16-17

Author / Source:
Ovid

Genre:
Myth

Cross-curricular links:
- History (Ancient Rome)

Introduction

Ovid is widely seen as one of the most important poets in Latin literature. His best-known work, the 15-book poem the *Metamorphoses*, is a key source of Ancient Greek and Roman mythology. *The Oak and the Linden Tree* comes from book 8 of the *Metamorphoses*. The story ends with Jupiter destroying Phrygia in a great flood. Only Philemon and Baucis are spared, and their humble hut becomes a beautiful temple. When the couple eventually die, they are turned into an oak tree and a linden tree, standing together where Phrygia used to be.

Answers

1. Any appropriate answer. E.g. Yes, because the text says that Mount Olympus was "perfect" and that the gods had plenty of food, music and stories. If I lived somewhere like that, I'd never want to leave. OR E.g. No, because the text says there was "nothing to do" on Mount Olympus, so I'm not surprised that Jupiter got bored and wanted to leave. I wouldn't want to stay in a place where there was nothing to do either.
2. E.g. To make himself look like a poor traveller.
3. E.g. Mercury and Jupiter go to Phrygia in disguise. They knock on doors asking for help, but everyone turns them away.
4. c. personification
5. E.g. It's about gods and it's set in ancient times.
6. Any appropriate answer. E.g. I think that Jupiter will punish the people of Phrygia who wouldn't help him, but he will reward Philemon and Baucis because they were kind to him.

Extra Activities

- Ask pupils to share their answers to question 5 in the Question Book, then discuss other typical features of myths. What are the similarities and differences between myths and legends?
- Drawing on their answers to question 6 in the Question Book, ask pupils to write the last few paragraphs of *The Oak and the Linden Tree*. Encourage them to write in a similar style to the extract.
- Tell pupils the traditional ending to *The Oak and the Linden Tree*. What do they think the message of the myth is? Are they surprised that Philemon and Baucis are turned into trees at the end? Do they think this is a good reward? Divide the class into groups and get pupils to compare the traditional ending with the endings they wrote themselves. Do they find the similarities and/or differences surprising? Which ending is their favourite, and why?
- Assign pupils different Roman gods. Ask them to find out what their god was responsible for and what their particular characteristics and powers were. Pupils should produce an illustrated fact sheet about their god — these could be used to create a classroom display based around Mount Olympus.
- Ask pupils to write their own Roman myth to explain the extinction of the dinosaurs. Their myths should have some of the typical features identified in the class discussion. Encourage them to include some of the Roman gods they have learned about.

Cora and the King

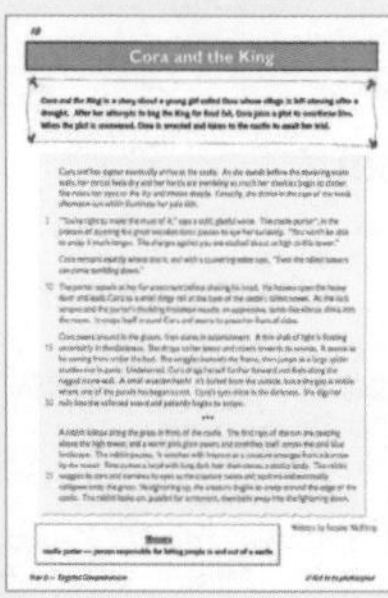

Question Book:
Year 5, pages 18-19

Author / Source:
Louise McEvoy

Genre:
Fiction — short story

Cross-curricular links:
- PSHE (peaceful protests)

Introduction

Cora and the King is a short story about a young woman called Cora and her involvement in a rebellion against a cruel king. This extract uses lots of figurative language to bring the setting to life. As pupils read the text, encourage them to identify examples of figurative language and to think about the effect they have on the reader.

Answers

1. E.g. Worried, because her "hands are trembling". Shaking hands are often a sign that someone is worried.
2. E.g. That even though she faces a lot of charges, there's still hope that she could get off.
3. Any appropriate answer. E.g. It makes the reader feel like the story is happening as they read it, which makes it more exciting.
4. c. onomatopoeia
5. E.g. It separates you from Cora when the action reaches its most exciting point. This creates tension because it makes you feel uncertain about what's happening to her.
6. E.g. Yes, because she's trying to help the poor and stop the King from treating people unfairly. I don't think she deserves to be in prison. OR E.g. No, because I think the story would be more exciting if she got captured again. The plot would be too predictable if she managed to escape this easily.

Extra Activities

- Ask pupils to underline examples of personification in the extract, then get them to suggest other techniques that the author could have used (e.g. similes, metaphors, onomatopoeia). As a class, discuss why authors use these techniques and the effect they have on the reader.
- Discuss what might happen to Cora, then ask pupils to write the next paragraph of the story. They should write in the present tense and use the techniques discussed in the first activity.
- Look at the verbs that describe the rabbit's behaviour in the final paragraph of the extract, e.g. "lollops", "waggles". Ask pupils to rewrite the final paragraph using a different animal, e.g. a bird. They should choose verbs that convey their animal's movements, e.g. a bird might 'flit', 'flutter' or 'glide'.
- Explain that a castle porter's responsibilities included guarding prisoners and letting people into and out of the castle. Ask pupils to write a set of instructions from the porter, explaining important 'dos' and 'don'ts' of the job, e.g. 'don't let in anyone you don't know', 'always keep the key to the tower around your neck'.
- In the story, Cora initially protests peacefully by begging the king for more food. Can pupils think of any other forms of peaceful protest (e.g. marches, sit-ins, boycotting something, writing a petition)? Why do pupils think some people might choose to protest in this way? Introduce pupils to an example of a successful peaceful protest, such as the Montgomery bus boycott of 1955-56. Are pupils surprised that peaceful protests can be effective?

Robot on the Ice

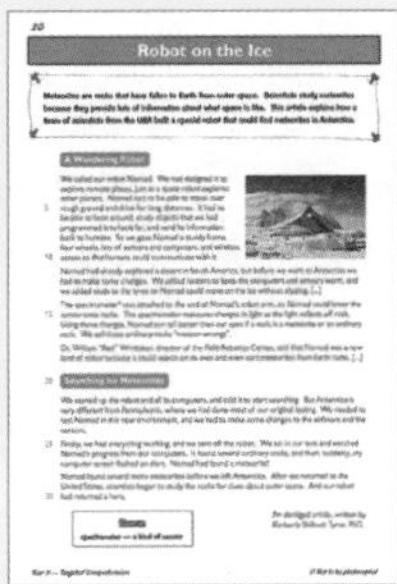

Question Book:
Year 5, pages 20-21

Author / Source:
Kimberly Shillcutt Tyree

Genre:
Non-fiction — news article

Cross-curricular links:
- Science (meteors)
- Geography (Antarctica)
- D&T (product design)

Introduction

This article focuses on Nomad, a "wandering robot" that helps NASA scientists to find meteorites in remote locations, such as Antarctica. It gives an insight into how this cutting-edge technology is designed, by explaining the features which help Nomad cope with the harsh Antarctic environment, and the instruments that enable it to find meteorites. Before pupils read the extract, show them some pictures of meteors and meteorites. Explain that meteors (also known as shooting stars) are the streaks of light we see when small pieces of space debris burn up in the Earth's atmosphere, while meteorites are pieces of space debris that have reached Earth.

Answers

1. E.g. Because they needed to make sure the snow and ice in Antarctica wouldn't stop it working.
2. E.g. Because it's a pun. They're looking for meteorites, which sounds like 'meteor-rights', and ordinary rocks are the "wrong" kind of rocks.
3. E.g. Excited. You can tell because she uses an exclamation mark in the sentence about it finding a meteorite.
4. Any appropriate answer. E.g. Yes, because it has sub-headings, which break the text up and make it easier to read. It also includes a picture, which helps you to imagine the landscape that Nomad was exploring.
5. Any appropriate answer. E.g. Because nomads travel around in remote places. This is similar to what Nomad does — it goes to remote places like Antarctica and travels around looking for meteorites.
6. Any appropriate answer. E.g. Yes, because Nomad has done something impressive that most people wouldn't be able to do. I think that makes it a hero. OR E.g. No, because heroes usually risk their lives to help people. Nomad wasn't in danger and it wasn't helping people, so I don't think it's a hero.

Extra Activities

- With the whole class, discuss pupils' answers to question 5. Do they think Nomad is a good name for the robot? Ask them to come up with alternative names and explain their reasoning.
- Get pupils to imagine that a meteorite has landed in the school playground. They should write a newspaper article reporting the event.
- Ask pupils to research and write a guide to meteor-spotting. Their guide should cover things like what meteors look like as they burn up in the atmosphere, the best times of year and weather conditions for spotting meteors, where to go to look for them, and any equipment that makes it easier to spot them.
- Divide the class into groups and ask each group to research a different feature of Antarctica (e.g. climate, landscape, animal life). Each group should share their findings with the class. Pupils could then use what they have learnt about Antarctica to produce a poster that will persuade tourists to visit the region.
- Suggest other challenging environments (e.g. a dense jungle or the bottom of the ocean) and ask pupils to explain how they would adapt Nomad's design to enable it to function in those conditions. Get pupils to produce a labelled diagram of their design, with short descriptions of the main features. Pupils could also build models of their designs.

Candara's Gift

Question Book:
Year 5, pages 22-23

Author / Source:
Jasper Cooper

Genre:
Fiction — novel extract

Cross-curricular links:
- Art (fantasy maps)

Introduction

Jasper Cooper became a writer when he was in his forties, having previously worked as a teacher and a professional tennis and squash coach. *Candara's Gift* is the first in Cooper's popular *Kingdom of Gems* trilogy, which was inspired by the bedtime stories Cooper used to tell his children. The novels are set in a highly detailed fantasy world, complete with its own history and geography. As pupils read this extract, encourage them to think about the way Cooper uses descriptive language to create the sinister mood of the text.

Answers

1. E.g. The plants wither when the Troubler walks past, which suggests he has magical powers.
2. E.g. watchful; on the lookout; attentive; alert
3. "It swept across the kingdom from the west, like a curtain drawn at the end of the day"
4. E.g. The Troubler is making them sleep.
5. a. personification
6. E.g. He uses negative words like "dreadful" and "brooding", and he says that the kingdom seems to be waiting for something "uninvited and unwanted".
7. E.g. To show that the character is going to cause problems in the kingdom.
8. Any appropriate answer. E.g. He might feel guilty for letting a Troubler get in by falling asleep when he was meant to be keeping watch. He might also feel worried about what the Troubler will do.

Extra Activities

- Ask pupils to share their answers to question 1, then get them to identify other fantasy novels they have read and to explain how they could tell that they belonged to the fantasy genre. Make a list of the features often used in fantasy novels.
- Drawing on their answers to question 8, get pupils to write a diary entry from Joog's point of view, describing his reaction when he wakes up to find that a Troubler has entered the Kingdom.
- Ask pupils to underline examples of descriptive language in the extract and to identify other examples of similes and personification, as well as alliteration. With the whole class, discuss the effect that Cooper's use of language has on the reader.
- Secretly assign pupils different moods (e.g. happy, excited, sad), then ask them to write the opening paragraph of a story, using descriptive and figurative language to create the assigned mood in their writing. Pupils should then swap their writing with a partner and try to guess the mood of their partner's paragraph, using examples to explain their guess.
- Challenge pupils to invent a setting for a fantasy story of their own. They should draw a map showing the main features of their fantasy world.

The Hound of the Baskervilles

24

The Hound of the Baskervilles

Question Book:
Year 5, pages 24-25

Author / Source:
Arthur Conan Doyle (adapted)

Genre:
Classic fiction — novel extract

Cross-curricular links:

- Geography (UK National Parks)

Introduction

Arthur Conan Doyle was born in Edinburgh in 1859. He worked as a doctor, and wrote many different genres, including non-fiction, poetry and plays, but he is most famous for his novels and short stories about the fictional detective Sherlock Holmes. In 1893, Conan Doyle tried to kill off Holmes, but due to public outcry he eventually brought the detective back in *The Hound of the Baskervilles*, which was serialised in 1901-2. In this story, Holmes and Watson are employed by Sir Henry Baskerville, who fears that the house he has inherited, Baskerville Hall on Dartmoor, is haunted by a huge, demonic hound. As pupils read the extract, encourage them to think about Conan Doyle's characterisation of Holmes and Watson.

Answers

1. He could see Watson in the polished coffee pot in front of him.
2. E.g. conclusions; possible answers
3. a. E.g. He feels pleased and proud because he thinks that Holmes is impressed by what he has worked out about Dr Mortimer. b. E.g. Yes. Holmes says that Watson actually got lots of things wrong, so Watson might feel a bit embarrassed.
4. E.g. Formal. It uses formal phrases like "a great deal" instead of "a lot", and Holmes says things like "you excel yourself", which sounds very formal.
5. Any appropriate answer. E.g. Clever, because he can work things out that Watson can't. Unkind, because he pretends that Watson is doing a good job, but then rudely tells him that he made lots of mistakes.

Extra Activities

- Ask pupils to identify features of this text that suggest it's a mystery story. Can they think of any other features of mystery stories?
- Discuss pupils' answers to question 5. Are their answers similar or different? Are they surprised that there are different interpretations of Holmes's personality? How would they describe Watson's personality? Encourage pupils to explain how Conan Doyle conveys these contrasting characters.
- Ask pupils to write a few paragraphs describing what they think happens next. Then encourage them to think about what they have learned about the characters and setting when writing their paragraphs.
- Get pupils to create their own fictional detective and write a profile of them. They should outline their detective's background, their skills, their personality traits and any other defining characteristics.
- *The Hound of the Baskervilles* is partly set on Dartmoor, one of the UK's National Parks (others include the Lake District, Snowdonia and the Cairngorms). Split the class into groups and assign each group a different National Park. The groups should research their park and prepare a presentation to persuade classmates that it is the best location for a school trip. Hold a vote on which group was most persuasive.

Harambe the Gorilla

Harambe the Gorilla

The only thing more upsetting than Harambe the gorilla's death was the reality of his life

Question Book:
Year 5, pages 26-27

Author / Source:
www.independent.co.uk

Genre:
Non-fiction — news article

Cross-curricular links:
- PSHE (animal welfare)
- Science (endangered species)

Introduction

People around the world were shocked by the shooting of Harambe the gorilla at Cincinnati Zoo in May 2016. For some, the incident raised questions not only about the security of zoo enclosures, but about the legitimacy of keeping animals in zoos at all. This article introduces pupils to issues relating to conservation, particularly the debate surrounding the best ways to protect endangered species. Before pupils read the text, ask them about their attitudes towards zoos — have they ever visited a zoo? Did they enjoy it? Do they think that zoos are a good idea?

Answers

1. E.g. Because it suggests that being in a zoo is like being in prison. This makes the reader think that zoos are bad because it suggests that being in a zoo feels like a horrible punishment for the animals.
2. Animals should not be kept for people to gawk at in zoos. — Opinion
   The shooting of Harambe led to a lot of debate online. — Fact
   Zoo animals lead lives of quiet desperation. — Opinion (1 mark for 2 correct, 2 marks for all 3 correct)
3. E.g. Zoos say that they are trying to protect animals. However, zoos can be bad for wild animals because they use up funding that could be spent on protecting animals in the wild.
4. Any appropriate answer. E.g. I think the zoo was right because Harambe might have hurt or killed the boy if they hadn't shot him first. OR E.g. I think the zoo was wrong because they were supposed to be looking after Harambe. They should have found a way to rescue the boy without killing the gorilla.
5. Any appropriate answer. E.g. I think it's a bad idea because animals don't like being trapped in zoos — it's better for them to live freely in the wild. OR E.g. I think it's a good idea because zoos help people learn about wild animals, and this makes them more interested in trying to protect them.

Extra Activities

- Ask pupils to explain whether the article has affected their attitudes towards zoos. With the whole class, discuss the techniques the author uses to persuade the reader of her point of view, e.g. the use of "Surely" in the first paragraph, the first person plural "we", and emotive words like "upsetting" and "desperation".
- Get half the class to research the benefits of zoos, and half to research the arguments against them. Hold a class debate between the two groups.
- Assign pupils different endangered animals (e.g. black rhino, Sumatran orangutan, Amur leopard). Pupils should research their animal and produce an illustrated leaflet describing its behaviour, habitat and diet, and explaining why it is endangered. Then get pupils to swap their leaflet with a partner and give each other feedback. What was good about the leaflet? What could be done to improve it?
- Get pupils to find out about a conservation project that aims to protect their endangered animal. Ask them to write an article that will persuade people to support the project. Encourage pupils to use the persuasive techniques identified in the class discussion in their article.

The Highwayman

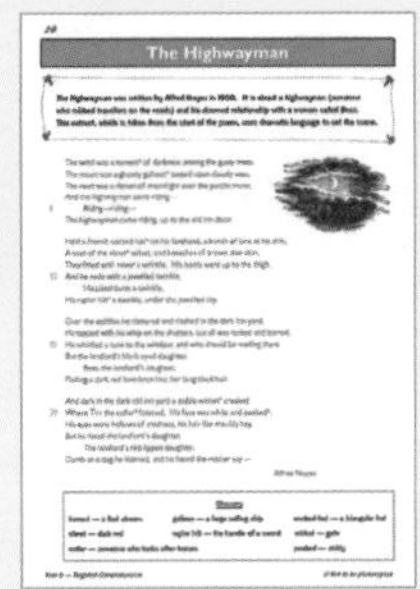

Question Book:
Year 5, pages 28-29

Author / Source:
Alfred Noyes

Genre:
Classic poetry

Cross-curricular links:
- Art (illustration)
- History (highwaymen)

Introduction

Alfred Noyes was a British poet and writer. Born in 1880, he was influenced by Romantic poets like Wordsworth, and by the narrative poetry of Tennyson. *The Highwayman* is one of Noyes' best-known poems. It is written in the form of a ballad, and draws on traditional English folk songs and stories. The poem uses vivid imagery to bring the setting and characters to life. Encourage pupils to read each stanza out loud so that they can appreciate the strong, driving rhythm of the poem.

Answers

1. c. AABCCB
2. "The wind was a torrent of darkness" OR "The moon was a ghostly galleon tossed upon cloudy seas" OR "The road was a ribbon of moonlight"
3. E.g. It helps the reader imagine how strong the wind is because it creates a picture of the moon being tossed around like a ship at sea. The word "ghostly" makes the reader think that the poem will be spooky.
4. E.g. the starry sky
5. d. alliteration
6. E.g. He uses horrible images like "mouldy hay" to describe the way he looks, and he describes Tim's eyes as "hollows of madness", which makes him sound unpleasant and frightening.
7. Any appropriate answer. E.g. Yes. The setting is dramatic and the characters sound interesting, so I think something exciting will happen in the poem. I want to keep reading to find out what happens.

Extra Activities

- Drawing on pupils' answers to question 3, discuss how the metaphors in the first stanza set the scene and mood of the poem. Ask pupils to think of their own metaphors to describe the scene and create a similar mood. Suggest some contrasting settings (e.g. a birthday party, a spring morning), and ask pupils to come up with metaphors to describe these scenes and create a suitable mood.
- With the whole class, explore how Noyes uses rhyme and repetition to create a rhythm that mirrors the sound of horses' hooves. Why do they think Noyes chose this rhythm for the poem?
- Get pupils to write the first two stanzas of their own narrative poem. Their stanzas should create a strong mood and introduce the main character. Encourage pupils to use some of the techniques discussed in the activities above, such as metaphors, rhythm and rhyme scheme.
- Ask pupils to draw an annotated picture of the highwayman. They should use the information in the second stanza and infer details from the rest of the poem.
- Divide the class into groups and assign each group a question about highwaymen (e.g. What did highwaymen do? How were they punished? Who were some famous highwaymen?). Pupils should research their question and then share their findings with the class.

Steve Jobs' Biography

Question Book:
Year 5, pages 30-31

Author / Source:
Karen Blumenthal

Genre:
Non-fiction — biography

Cross-curricular links:
- PSHE (failure)

Introduction

Steve Jobs co-founded Apple in 1976 and played a major role in designing the company's early PCs. In 1985, he fell out with Apple's CEO, John Sculley, and was stripped of his managerial duties. He worked on other projects for over a decade, but in 1997 he returned to Apple, where his unique design ethos became central to the creation of the company's successful range of MP3 players, smartphones and tablet computers. This text gives pupils an insight into Jobs' complex personality and describes some of the highs and lows of his career.

Answers

1. E.g. It is written in the third person, not in the first person.
2. E.g. developed; supported; looked after
3. E.g. Yes. She uses very positive language to describe them. For example, she calls Pixar's movies "amazing" and says Steve helped to make "insanely awesome technology".
4. Any appropriate answer. E.g. He might have felt angry about having his responsibilities taken away from him in a company that he co-founded. He might also have been worried about whether he would be able to find another job and support himself.
5. E.g. The individual words are separated by full stops. She might have done this to make the words stand out and to emphasise how different they are.
6. Any appropriate answer. E.g. Yes, because I enjoy using the technology he worked on, so it would have been really interesting to meet him and to learn about how he designed the different products. OR E.g. No, because the text describes him as "difficult" and says he got upset when things didn't go well for him, so I don't think I would have got on with him.

Extra Activities

- With the whole class, discuss the features of biographies. Make a list of the similarities and differences between biographies and autobiographies.
- Split the class into pairs. Each pupil should write a short biography outlining Steve Jobs' achievements. They should then share their biography with their partner and discuss what they wrote. Was there something their partner included that they missed? Encourage pupils to make changes to their work based on their discussion with their partner.
- With the whole class, discuss the meaning of the word "failure". Do pupils see it as something positive or negative? Explain to the class that Jobs believed being forced to leave Apple was the best thing that ever happened to him. Are they surprised? What does this tell them about Jobs' attitude towards failure? Challenge pupils to come up with strategies for turning apparent failure into something positive.
- Ask pupils to think of an electronic device that they've used at home or at school. Ask them to research their chosen device and make an advert to promote it. Pupils should include the product's innovative features, and present them in an eye-catching and persuasive way.

Talking Turkeys!!

Question Book:
Year 6, pages 2-3

Author / Source:
Benjamin Zephaniah

Genre:
Poetry

Cross-curricular links:

- PSHE (reducing waste; animal welfare)

Introduction

Talking Turkeys!! is taken from Zephaniah's first collection of children's poetry, which was originally published in 1994. *Talking Turkeys!!* is a fun and engaging poem for children, with some strong messages about animal rights and consumerism. A lot of Zephaniah's poetry is designed to be heard, rather than read, and children may enjoy listening to a video clip of Zephaniah performing his poem after they have read it.

Answers

1. E.g. Turkeys have the right to life, the right to roam freely and the right to not be genetically modified.
2. d. ABCBDED
3. E.g. Benjamin uses some non-standard spellings such as "yu" and "dis". I think he chose to do this because it reflects his own accent.
4. a. d. personification b. E.g. Because it gives the turkey a voice, so the reader sympathises with it.
5. E.g. I don't think Benjamin likes Christmas because it's a time when people eat turkeys. He also says that humans are "greedy" and wasteful at Christmas.
6. Any appropriate answer. E.g. No, because eating turkey at Christmas is traditional and Christmas dinner wouldn't be the same without some turkey. OR E.g. Yes, because thinking about Christmas from the turkey's perspective makes me feel guilty. We don't need to eat them — there's plenty of other food.

Extra Activities

- Explain to the class what a half-rhyme is. Ask pupils to identify all the half-rhymes in the poem.
- Point out lines 20-21 and explain that they form a rhetorical question. As a class, discuss how this technique affects the reader. Why do pupils think authors use rhetorical questions in persuasive writing?
- Ask pupils to write a poem entitled *Talking Trees!!* about Christmas trees that don't want to be cut down. Pupils should write in a similar style to *Talking Turkeys!!* and use features they've learnt, e.g. half-rhymes, rhetorical questions and phonetic spellings. Ask some pupils to perform their poems to the class.
- Initiate a discussion about Christmas. Zephaniah raises the issues of waste (people cutting down Christmas trees) and greed (business people exploiting consumers at Christmas time). Do pupils feel differently about Christmas after reading the poem? In response to this, ask pupils to produce a leaflet that explains how families can reduce waste at Christmas time.
- Split pupils into small groups and ask them to research what people from other countries and cultures eat at Christmas time. Ask pupils to present their findings to the rest of the class.
- Explain to pupils that some poultry farmers rear birds indoors with very little space. Other farmers rear free-range poultry instead, which means that the birds have access to outdoor areas. Get pupils to draw up a table of pros and cons for free-range and indoor-reared poultry. Then, split the class in half and hold a debate between the two groups about whether all poultry should be free-range.

Pig Heart Boy

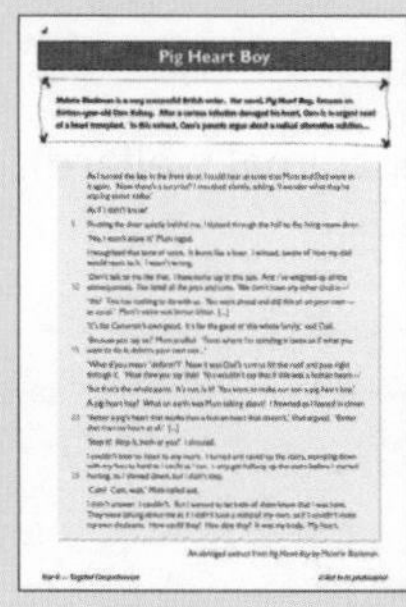

Question Book:
Year 6, pages 4-5

Author / Source:
Malorie Blackman

Genre:
Fiction — novel extract

Cross-curricular links:

- PSHE (medical ethics)
- Science (the heart)
- PE (exercise and heart rate)
- Maths (line graphs)

Introduction

Malorie Blackman has written numerous novels for children and young adults. Her novels often use science fiction to tackle complex ethical issues. *Pig Heart Boy* explores the issues that could arise from the use of pig organs for human transplants. Before pupils read the extract, make sure they are aware that the transplantation of whole organs from pigs to humans is not currently possible. You may also want to explain that heart valves from pigs and cows can be used to replace damaged human heart valves, and that scientists in the USA are attempting to grow human organs in pigs for transplantation.

Answers

1. "Now there's a surprise!" OR "I wonder what they're arguing about today."
2. "It burnt like a laser"
3. E.g. To show that Cam's mum stressed those words when she spoke. It also helps to emphasise that she's angry with Cam's dad for making up his mind about the pig heart treatment without asking her.
4. E.g. The dialogue makes the extract feel realistic. It also helps the reader to understand the characters better because it shows how Cam's parents feel about the situation.
5. Any appropriate answer. E.g. He feels angry with his parents for making decisions about his treatment without asking him first. He might also feel upset that his parents have been arguing.
6. Any appropriate answer. E.g. Yes, because Cam's own heart doesn't work properly — he can't even run all the way up the stairs. If he has the transplant then he might be able to lead a more normal life. OR E.g. No, I think that Cam should wait for a human heart because using a pig's heart might be more likely to have complications, and Cam's mum says that it would "deform" him.

Extra Activities

- As a class, discuss the use of direct speech in this extract. Do pupils enjoy reading texts that use a lot of direct speech? Get pupils to underline all the words that Blackman uses instead of "said". How many other words can they think of that they could use instead of "said"?
- Ask pupils to write a short dialogue between two friends who have fallen out. Encourage them to use the techniques identified in the class discussion to make their dialogue interesting and to avoid repetition.
- Hold a class debate about the idea of using animal organs to treat people who need organ transplants.
- Explain to the class how blood circulates between the heart, the lungs and the rest of the body. Give pupils a diagram of the heart and challenge them to find out the names of the different chambers and blood vessels. Can they add arrows to show the circulation of blood around the heart?
- Get pupils to measure their resting heart rate, then give them a list of activities, such as star jumps, running on the spot and balancing on one leg. Ask pupils to do each activity for one minute and measure their heart rate immediately afterwards, one minute later and two minutes later. They should then draw line graphs to show how each activity affected their heart rate.

The Story of My Life

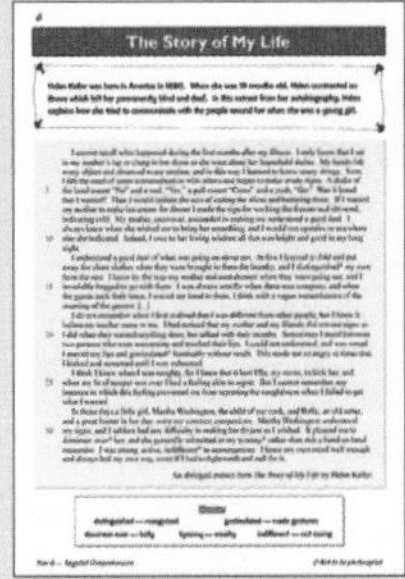

Question Book:
Year 6, pages 6-7

Author / Source:
Helen Keller

Genre:
Non-fiction — autobiography

Cross-curricular links:
- PSHE (disability; braille)

Introduction

Helen Keller (1880-1968) had a remarkable life and most children will find her story fascinating. Although Helen was blind and deaf, her tutor, Anne Sullivan, taught her how to communicate, and the pair remained very close until Sullivan's death in 1936. Helen attended several specialised educational institutions and successfully earned a degree in 1904. Today, Helen is still remembered for her achievements; she has appeared on American currency and stamps, and has lent her name to streets, hospitals and schools.

Answers

1. E.g. It is written in the first person. It recalls events from Helen's life.
2. E.g. I think it means Helen's blindness. Because she can't see, there is only darkness.
3. E.g. Because she remembered waving to guests before her illness.
4. E.g. Because Helen knew she would get what she wanted if she kicked her nurse. Helen also felt angry and frustrated at not being able to speak and this was how she let out her anger.
5. E.g. Helen admits she was very mean to Martha, so Martha probably didn't like Helen very much. She was probably also scared of Helen, because Helen says that Martha nearly always did what Helen wanted her to do.
6. Any appropriate answer. E.g. If I was blind and deaf I wouldn't be able to do a lot of the things I like to do, like listen to music and play football. I wouldn't have any independence because I would probably need someone to help me do simple things like go to the shops or cross the road.

Extra Activities

- Discuss the differences between autobiographical and biographical writing. Ask pupils to research important events in Helen Keller's life, e.g. meeting her teacher Anne Sullivan for the first time, going to college, receiving her degree, meeting Winston Churchill etc. Then ask pupils to write an account of one of the events they've researched in a biographical style.
- Drawing on pupils' research for the first activity, discuss whether they think Helen Keller's disability held her back. Are pupils surprised that she achieved so much? Do pupils think Helen's life would have been different if she hadn't lost her hearing and her sight?
- Explain to pupils that a play called *The Miracle Worker* was made about Helen Keller and her teacher, Anne Sullivan. The events in it were based on events from Helen Keller's autobiography. Ask pupils to re-read the final paragraph of the extract, then write a playscript for a scene in which Helen and Martha Washington play together as children.
- Helen could read braille. Introduce children to the braille alphabet. Can pupils write their name in braille (by colouring in the dots rather than raising them)? Divide pupils into pairs, then ask each pupil to write their own message in braille. Pupils should swap messages with their partner, then decipher the one they receive.

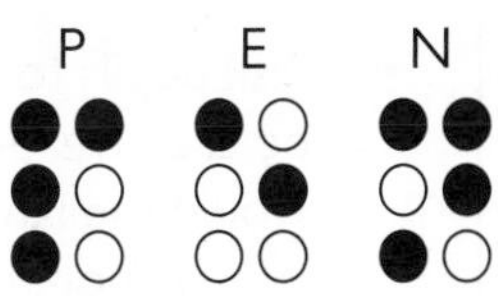

The Lost Diary of Snow White

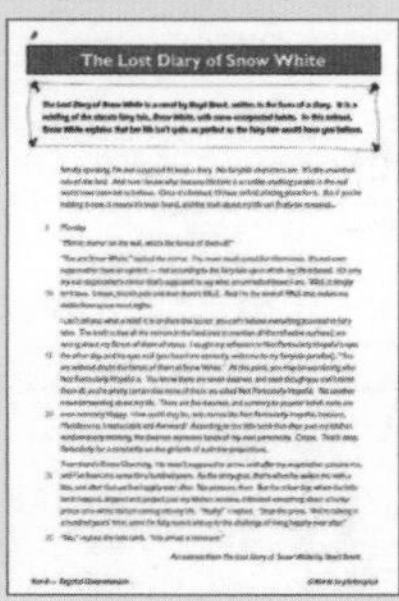
The Lost Diary of Snow White

Question Book:
Year 6, pages 8-9

Author / Source:
Boyd Brent

Genre:
Fiction — novel extract

Cross-curricular links:

- D&T (costume and set design)

Introduction

Pupils will almost certainly be familiar with the story of Snow White, but this modernised version is told from the perspective of Snow White in the form of a diary. Both boys and girls will enjoy the witty writing style, as well as the inversion of some of the classic fairytale elements. Before reading the text, ask pupils to explain what they know about the plot and characters of the tale of Snow White.

Answers

1. Any two from: it is written in the first person; the entry starts with "Monday"; it contains the writer's thoughts and feelings; it talks about events that happened that day; it uses informal language; it has a chatty tone.
2. E.g. To make it stand out, which emphasises just how pale Snow White is.
3. E.g. "welcome to my fairytale paradise"
4. E.g. The names of the dwarves represent Snow White's personality, so she's pessimistic, unsure, interfering, sad and awkward.
5. E.g. Most traditional fairy tales use quite formal language. The language in this story is a lot more informal and chatty, for example "Cripes" and "No pressure, then".
6. E.g. No, because she says she needs to rest for a hundred years to be "up to the challenge", which suggests that she is reluctant about living happily ever after.

Extra Activities

- Initiate a discussion about whether pupils prefer this version of Snow White or the traditional version. Ask pupils to write a review of this version of Snow White, explaining the reasons for their preference.
- Explain to pupils that irony can be shown through language (for example, their answer to Q3) as well as through situations. Give pupils the following definition of situational irony: "when readers' expectations don't match up with what actually happens in the story." Challenge pupils to find some examples of situational irony from the text (e.g. Snow White's "fairytale" life isn't actually much of a fairy tale).
- Ask pupils to write a diary entry from the perspective of a different fairytale character, e.g. Sleeping Beauty, Prince Charming, Cinderella. Ask them to invert some of the traditional features of those characters and their stories. For example, what if Prince Charming was actually quite rude or if Cinderella was just as lazy as her ugly sisters?
- Ask pupils to design the scenery and costumes for a stage version of this extract. Encourage pupils to be creative — if life in Snow White's fairytale land is different to the traditional version of the story, would the landscape and clothes look different as well? Pupils should label their drawings with useful information, e.g. materials to be used, a rough estimate of size.

The Yellow Train

Question Book:
Year 6, pages 10-11

Author / Source:
www.telegraph.co.uk

Genre:
Non-fiction — travel article

Cross-curricular links:
- Geography (the Pyrenees)
- Art (Charles Rennie Mackintosh)
- Science (circuit diagrams)

Introduction

Officially opened to the public in 1909, the Yellow Train remains a popular tourist attraction in the south of France. This travel article uses poetic and imaginative descriptions to recreate the character and charm of the Yellow Train, whilst delivering useful factual information to readers. Before reading the article, show pupils some images of the Pyrenees and ask them if they would like to go there.

Answers

1. E.g. Because the train isn't like modern trains, so it's like going back in time.
2. E.g. A symphony is where all the different instruments in an orchestra feature in a piece of music. I think the author is saying that the Yellow Train's surroundings are made up of lots of different natural features.
3. b. a metaphor
4. a. c. to inform   b. E.g. Because it contains facts which tell the reader about the train journey.
5. Any appropriate answer. E.g. Different, because the newspapers that I've read usually talk about current affairs, not travel. They also don't use as much descriptive language. OR E.g. Similar, because it is a non-fiction text that gives information about something.
6. Any appropriate answer. E.g. Yes, because the article makes a journey on the Yellow Train sound like an amazing experience, for example the author calls it a "magical trip". OR E.g. No, because I don't like heights and the article describes part of the train journey as being like "the roof of the world".

Extra Activities

- Split the class into groups. Ask each group to underline examples of descriptive language in the extract (e.g. "magical trip", "tumultuous scenery"). As a class, discuss the effect of this language on the reader. Compile this descriptive language into a class display to help pupils with their own creative writing.
- Get pupils to imagine they are going on a train journey to an amazing place (either real or fictional). They should write their own travel article about the trip, making the scenery sound as attractive as possible.
- Show pupils a map of Europe and ask them to use the introduction in the Question Book to locate the Pyrenees. Ask pupils to research how the range was formed, the climate and popular tourist locations and activities. Pupils should use their research to create a tourist leaflet for the Pyrenees.
- Charles Rennie Mackintosh was a famous Scottish artist and architect, born in 1868. He moved to the south of France in the 1920s and lived in a town called Port-Vendres. Get pupils to research Mackintosh's watercolours of Port-Vendres. Pupils should consider his use of colour and shape, then create a watercolour painting of their own in a similar style.
- Explain to pupils that the Yellow Train is powered by electricity. Show pupils an image of a simple electric circuit, then ask them to write a set of instructions describing how to set one up. Pupils should then swap their work with a partner and advise each other on how it could be improved.

David Copperfield

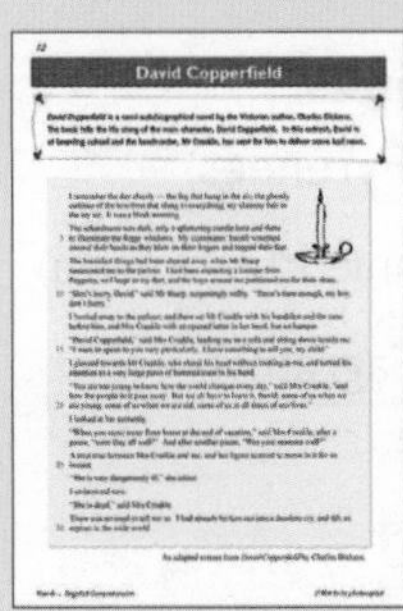

Question Book:
Year 6, pages 12-13

Author / Source:
Charles Dickens (adapted)

Genre:
Classic fiction — novel extract

Cross-curricular links:
- History (Victorian Britain)
- Drama (stage directions)

Introduction

This extract from *David Copperfield* has been adapted to make it more accessible to Year 6 pupils, but it still retains much of Dickens' original language and his distinctive writing style. *David Copperfield* tells the story of its titular character through retrospective narration. This extract is from an early part of the novel, when David is told that his mother has died. To draw attention to the way Dickens sets the scene, pause after reading the first paragraph and ask pupils to predict whether something good or bad might happen to David.

Answers

1. E.g. The text is partly based on real events from Charles Dickens' life and partly fictional.
2. E.g. Words like "ghostly" and "bleak" make the setting seem lonely and depressing. The author chose this setting to create a suitable mood for the bad news David is about to receive.
3. E.g. The phrase "surprisingly softly" suggests that Mr Sharp is usually quite blunt.
4. E.g. Mrs Creakle feels sad and uncomfortable. She is sad because David's mother has died, but she also feels uncomfortable because she has to break the news to David.
5. E.g. The "mist" is tears forming in David's eyes, which are stopping him from seeing properly.
6. E.g. hopeless; miserable; bleak; dismal
7. E.g. Candles are used to light the room rather than electric lights. The extract uses old-fashioned language like "parlour" and "mamma". The news of David's mother's death was sent by letter, rather than by a phone call or an email.

Extra Activities

- Drawing on pupils' answers to question 7 and other details in the text, challenge pupils to work out what time period *David Copperfield* is set in. As a class, discuss how life for a child like David in Victorian Britain might have been different to daily life for children today.
- Ask pupils to rewrite the first two paragraphs of the extract so that it has a bright and cheery tone. Pupils should retain key elements of the text, e.g. they should use first person narration, write in the past tense and use the setting of a classroom.
- Get pupils to write a letter from Mrs Creakle to Peggotty, David's old nurse, describing David's reaction when he heard that his mother had died and how he has been coping in the days following the news.
- Ask pupils to imagine they are directing this extract in a stage version of *David Copperfield*. They should re-write the extract as a playscript, adding in their own stage directions. Encourage pupils to think about lighting, sound effects and the position of the characters on the stage.
- Victorian schoolchildren like David would have learnt to write in a type of handwriting called copperplate. Show children some phrases written in copperplate and ask them to try to copy them in the same style.

Edible Cutlery

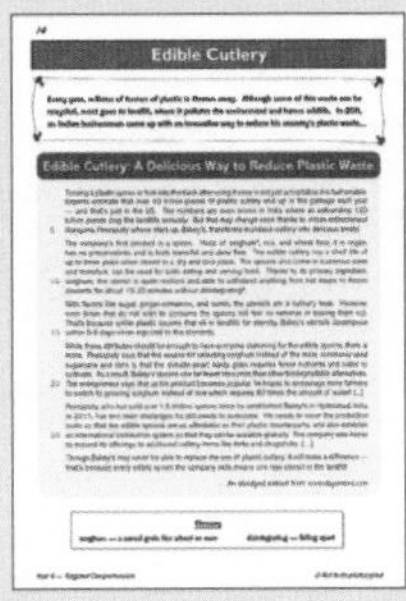

Question Book:
Year 6, pages 14-15

Author / Source:
www.dogonews.com

Genre:
Non-fiction — news article

Cross-curricular links:
- PSHE (protecting the environment)
- Science (properties of materials)
- Maths (percentages; pie charts)

Introduction

Edible cutlery is an original idea launched by an Indian company, Bakey's, to create an eco-friendly alternative to disposable plastic cutlery. This article explains the ideas behind the design and development of the edible cutlery, which Bakey's hopes to launch on a global scale. Their unique idea should engage pupils and inspire them to think about innovative ways of being environmentally friendly.

Answers

1. E.g. The spoons come in several tasty flavours. If people throw the spoons away instead of eating them, it doesn't stop them from being environmentally friendly. The spoons will quickly decompose.
2. E.g. Imaginative, because he has created a clever, original solution to the problem of plastic cutlery.
3. Bakey's utensils decompose within 5-6 days when exposed to the elements. — Fact
   Tossing a plastic spoon into the trash is fashionable. — Opinion
   The utensils are a culinary treat. — Opinion (1 mark for 2 correct, 2 marks for all 3 correct)
4. Any appropriate answer. E.g. Yes, the author thinks the spoons are a good idea (she calls them "delicious treats"), so the article is unbalanced because it concentrates on the positive aspects of the products and the company. OR E.g. No, although the author mentions a lot of positive things about the spoons and the company, she also mentions some of the problems that the business faces, so the article isn't biased.
5. Any appropriate answer. E.g. No, because plastic cutlery is more practical and can be used in lots of different situations. Plastic cutlery lasts forever, but edible cutlery goes off. OR E.g. Yes, because once it's cheaper and more widely available, I think lots of people will want to buy edible cutlery.

Extra Activities

- Imagine that Bakey's are launching their edible cutlery in the UK. Ask pupils to write a script for a TV advert promoting the edible spoons. The advert should be informative and persuasive. Pupils might also want to create a jingle or a catchy slogan. Pupils could perform their adverts to the rest of the class.
- Ask pupils to create an eco-friendly superhero with green superpowers. For example, it could use solar energy to fly and have the ability to ingest greenhouse gases. Pupils should draw and label their superhero, then write a short paragraph describing how their powers will help them to save the planet.
- Ask pupils to think about the properties that Bakey's spoons need to have in order to be fit for purpose (e.g. they need to be rigid, fairly insoluble, biodegradable). Conduct an investigation to test whether there is another material which could be used to make an environmentally-friendly spoon.
- The article mentions that the edible spoons come in different flavours, e.g. sugar, ginger-cinammon and cumin. Inform pupils that garlic and plain spoons are also on sale. Conduct a survey amongst the class about which flavour pupils would like to try. Pupils should work out what percentage of the class would like to try each flavour (to the nearest 1%), then create a pie chart to show their findings.

The Curse of the Gloamglozer

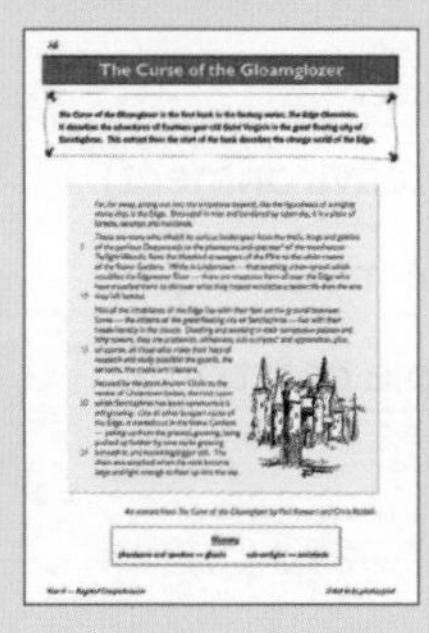

Question Book:
Year 6, pages 16-17

Author / Source:
Paul Stewart
Chris Riddell

Genre:
Fiction — novel extract

Cross-curricular links:

- Art (making a collage)
- History (place names)

Introduction

The Edge is an immersive and engaging world created by Paul Stewart and Chris Riddell in their fantasy series, *The Edge Chronicles*. The series spans 600 years of fictional history and includes maps, illustrations and vivid descriptions that bring the fictional world to life. Before reading the text with the class, discuss what they know about the fantasy genre and the types of characters they might expect to meet.

Answers

1. "jutting out into the emptiness beyond, like the figurehead of a mighty stone ship"
2. E.g. dangerous; unsafe; hazardous
3. E.g. To emphasise that the people of Sanctaphrax live very high up. The phrase also means that you don't really notice what's going on around you, so they might have chosen it to show that the people of Sanctaphrax don't pay much attention to what's happening below them in Undertown.
4. Any appropriate answer. E.g. I'd prefer to live in Sanctaphrax because it sounds so different to Earth. It floats and the people there live in towers and palaces. OR E.g. I'd prefer to live in Undertown because it's urban and I like cities. It also sounds like you'd get to meet lots of different creatures there.
5. E.g. The passage contains lots of description so it helps to create a clear picture of the setting in the reader's mind. It's important to explain the setting at the start of the book because it's so different to real life.
6. Any appropriate answer. E.g. An advantage is that you'd always have someone to discuss your ideas with if you got stuck. A disadvantage is that you might disagree about what should happen in the story.

Extra Activities

- Ask pupils to identify differences between the Edge and Earth, e.g. there are "trolls, trogs and goblins" on the Edge. Using these differences as a starting point, get pupils to invent more information about the Edge. They should produce a fact file describing the weather, sports, music and language on the Edge.
- Explain that fantasy fiction often takes an ordinary character and puts them in an extraordinary world. Ask pupils to work in pairs to write the opening page of a fantasy novel, where an ordinary character from Earth meets some stereotypical fantasy creatures, e.g. ghosts, trolls, goblins, dragons. Afterwards, discuss the positives and negatives that pupils experienced when writing a story with a partner.
- Challenge pupils to think of other examples of fantasy fiction, e.g. *Harry Potter, The Chronicles of Narnia*. As a class, see if pupils can identify any other common features of fantasy novels. Then ask pupils to create a poster displaying the different elements of the genre.
- Get pupils to make a collage of the Edge based on the extract, encouraging them to be creative with their choice of materials. Then ask pupils to compare their collages with a map of the Edge from the Internet.
- Discuss the place names mentioned in the extract. Ask the pupils if they can guess the reason behind any of the names, e.g. Undertown. Get pupils to research the origins of place names in their local area, e.g. 'Oxford' is derived from 'the ford where the oxen cross'.

Malala Yousafzai

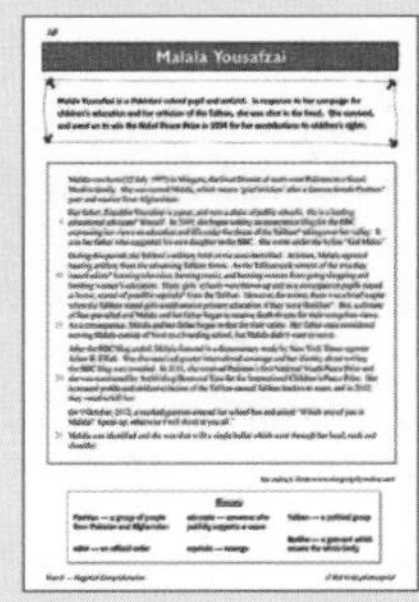

Question Book:
Year 6, pages 18-19

Author / Source:
www.biographyonline.net

Genre:
Non-fiction — biography

Cross-curricular links:
- PSHE (human rights)
- Geography (rivers)

Introduction

The true story of Malala Yousafzai and her fight to uphold human rights whilst living under the Taliban is inspirational. This biography explores Malala's early activism, when she wrote an anonymous blog for the BBC and became increasingly critical of the Taliban's regime in Pakistan. The extract is an ideal springboard for wider discussions about the importance of education and gender equality.

Answers

1. E.g. Because if the Taliban found out who she was then she'd be in danger.
2. E.g. Because she didn't want to give in to pressure from the Taliban. She might also have been scared to move away from her friends and family.
3. E.g. She might have felt happy because her work was becoming more well known, but also scared because it would be easier for the Taliban to find her and prevent her from speaking out against them.
4. E.g. harsh; bold
5. Any appropriate answer. E.g. Yes, because if Malala hadn't written the blog then she wouldn't have become such a well-known opponent of the Taliban, so they probably wouldn't have shot her. OR E.g. No, because the blog allowed Malala to raise awareness of the cruelty of the Taliban's regime and win the International Children's Peace Prize. Her father's decision helped her to become an international hero.
6. Any appropriate answer. E.g. Yes, because she has experienced a lot of hardship and pain. She has been persecuted and was nearly murdered by the Taliban. OR E.g. No. Although some terrible things have happened to her, she has also achieved some amazing things and never seems to have given up hope.

Extra Activities

- The extract ends on a cliffhanger. Ask pupils to research what happened to Malala after she was shot, and write up the information in the form of a biography.
- Malala was awarded the Nobel Peace Prize in 2014. Ask pupils to research other Nobel Peace Prize winners and choose one that they find particularly inspirational. Divide the class into pairs. Pupils should imagine they're going to interview their chosen winner and create a list of questions they would like to ask them. Get pupils to swap questions, research the answers and complete their partner's interview.
- As a class, discuss why pupils think Malala was willing to take such risks for education. Is the right to go to school something worth fighting for? Ask pupils to think of something they would fight for (e.g. gender equality, freedom of speech, racial equality) and get them to write their own blog post about it. Tell pupils that their blog post doesn't have to be based on personal experience.
- Ask pupils to identify Pakistan on a map. Point out the location of the Swat Valley, where Malala grew up. Explain that a huge river runs through the area. Give pupils a list of key terminology to do with rivers, e.g. source, mouth, tributaries, valley. Pupils should create an informative poster about the River Swat, which uses each word on the list.

Poems about World War One

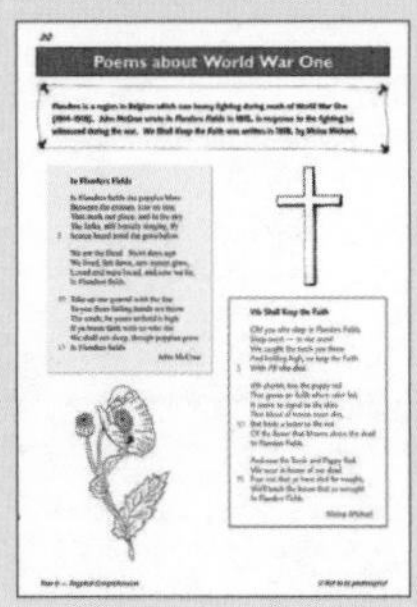

Question Book:
Year 6, pages 20-21

Author / Source:
John McCrae
Moina Michael

Genre:
Poetry

Cross-curricular links:
- History (World War One)
- PSHE (role models)
- Art (modern art)

Introduction

In Flanders Fields is one of the most enduring poems of the First World War. John McCrae wrote it after his friend, Alexis Helmer, died in battle in 1915. American professor Moina Michael wrote *We Shall Keep the Faith* in 1918 as a response to McCrae's poem. Both poems address the same subject from different perspectives. Before reading the poems, ensure pupils understand where Flanders is and the part it played in the war.

Answers

1. E.g. The graves of dead soldiers.
2. "Scarce heard amid the guns below"
3. E.g. It represents the cause that the soldiers were fighting for.
4. E.g. Because the poppies are red, which is the same colour as the soldiers' blood.
5. E.g. treasure; honour; value; love
6. E.g. She wanted to reassure people that the death and destruction caused by the war wasn't pointless. She promises that people will remember the soldiers who died.
7. Any appropriate answer. E.g. Yes, because wearing a poppy is a way of showing that we haven't forgotten about the soldiers who gave their lives for us. OR E.g. No, because we have other ways of remembering the soldiers, like museums. You can show respect in lots of different ways — not just by wearing a poppy.

Extra Activities

- With pupils, discuss the rhyme schemes of both poems. What do they notice about the line "In Flanders Fields"? (It is repeated within the poems and across the poems; it doesn't rhyme with the other lines in the poems.) Why do pupils think the line is repeated and why did the poets choose not to make it rhyme? (E.g. to make it stand out so that it is memorable, just like the soldiers who died.)
- Split pupils into pairs and ask each pair to write a sentence about how the punctuation affects the rhythm in line 6 of *In Flanders Fields* and line 2 of *We Shall Keep the Faith*. As a class, discuss pupils' responses. Why did the poets interrupt the rhythm here? (E.g. to emphasise the words "Dead" and "to rise anew".)
- Ask pupils who they think is speaking in each poem, then split the class in two. Ask one half to rewrite McCrae's poem as a letter, from the soldiers to future generations. Ask the other half to rewrite Michael's poem as a letter, from those who survived the war to the fallen soldiers.
- Get pupils to write their own poem about a person they admire. Before writing their poems, advise pupils to make a list of what they admire about their chosen figure and why.
- Show pupils examples of recent artworks designed to commemorate the First World War, e.g. the 'Blood Swept Lands and Seas of Red' installation at the Tower of London and 'The Face of World War One' project by Helen Marshall. Ask pupils to design their own memorial, presenting their work as a labelled drawing with a short paragraph explaining the ideas behind their design.

Moonfleet

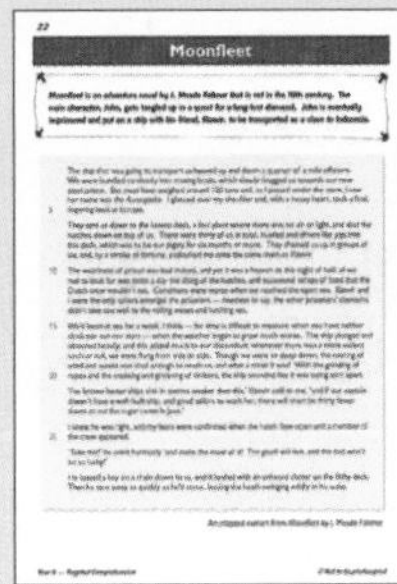

Question Book:
Year 6, pages 22-23

Author / Source:
J. Meade Falkner (adapted)

Genre:
Classic fiction — novel extract

Cross-curricular links:
- Science (astronomy)

Introduction

John Meade Falkner was an English writer and poet, born in 1858. *Moonfleet* is one of Falkner's most famous works and is a classic children's adventure story about smuggling. The story has been the basis of several television and film adaptations, including a BBC version broadcast in 1964 called *Smuggler's Bay*. In this extract, the protagonist, John, is being transported as a prisoner to Java when the ship he's travelling in gets caught in a storm. Before giving pupils the text, explain that the transportation of prisoners to overseas colonies was common in the 18th century and that the journeys were often long and dangerous.

Answers

1. E.g. disgusting; nasty; dirty; vile
2. a. d. a metaphor
   b. E.g. To show that the conditions on the lowest deck are smelly and unpleasant, like a pigsty.
3. E.g. Being in prison. He says that prison "was a heaven" compared to "this night of hell" on the ship.
4. E.g. John is in a dangerous situation. It's about an exciting quest for a long-lost diamond.
5. E.g. There are lots of exciting verbs like "plunged" and "flung". The author also uses onomatopoeia like "groaning" and "creaking", which makes the action very vivid.
6. Any appropriate answer. E.g. I think the ship will sink, but the narrator and Elzevir will survive because they're sailors and would know how to escape from a sinking ship.

Extra Activities

- Remind pupils what onomatopoeia is. Ask them to underline all the onomatopoeic words in the extract, e.g. "roaring" (line 18). Get pupils to write a description of a ship as it anchors at a busy port. They should use onomatopoeia to make their descriptions as vivid as possible.
- Explain that adventure stories often involve a 'problem' that characters solve by having an adventure. Ask pupils to identify the problem that John faces (being trapped on a sinking ship) and discuss how he might escape. Make a list of other 'problems' that could form the basis of an adventure story.
- Ask pupils to choose one of the 'problems' from the previous activity and use it to write their own adventure story. Before pupils start to write, they should plan their story. Encourage them to think about who their main characters will be and how the problem will be resolved.
- Ask pupils what they think the word "fleet" means. Explain that this is an example of a collective noun. Challenge pupils to write down one collective noun for each letter of the alphabet, e.g. an army of soldiers, a bunch of flowers, a caravan of camels etc. Their work could be turned into a wall display.
- Explain that some sailors in the northern hemisphere used to navigate using the North Star (Polaris). The North Star would always show them which direction they were travelling in because it is situated above the North Pole. Ask pupils to research how to locate the North Star in the night sky. They should draw and label a diagram of the North Star and the Plough to explain their findings.

Beowulf the Warrior

Question Book:
Year 6, pages 24-25

Author / Source:
Ian Serraillier

Genre:
Legend

Cross-curricular links:
- Drama (performance)
- History (Anglo-Saxons)
- Geography (Scandinavia)

Introduction

The legend of *Beowulf* is one of the oldest surviving poems written in Old English. It's an epic poem of over 3000 lines, which narrates the story of a heroic prince called Beowulf who saves King Hrothgar from an evil monster called Grendel and his mother. This extract will be engaging and exciting for pupils, as it sets the scene for a classic battle between good and evil. One of many modern translations, Ian Serraillier's version is more accessible for children, but it might be helpful to explain some background to the poem before you begin.

Answers

1. "huge hall" OR "high to heaven"
2. E.g. dangerous; unsafe; untrustworthy; unstable
3. E.g. One night when Hrothgar's men are sleeping, Grendel breaks into Heorot and kidnaps over twenty men. He takes them back to his home and eats them.
4. E.g. Very sad, because the hall rang with the "grief of the great King". He might also feel humiliated, as he hasn't been able to stop Grendel from terrorising his people.
5. E.g. The author's use of language makes Grendel sound evil. Descriptions like "fiend from hell" and "red ferocious eyes" create a threatening tone, which contrasts with the happiness at the start of the extract.
6. Any appropriate answer. E.g. Yes, because I want to know what happens to Grendel. I don't think he'll get away with killing so many people. The poem is also very exciting so it makes me want to read more.

Extra Activities

- Ask pupils to underline all the alliteration in the extract. As a class, discuss what effect it has on the rhythm. Lines 16-21 don't have any alliteration at all — why do pupils think the author did this?
- Tell the class the features of epic poetry (e.g. a long narrative poem that is usually about heroes and adventures). Ask them to rewrite an extract from a legend of their choosing, for example Robin Hood or an Arthurian legend, as an epic poem. Encourage them to use alliteration where they can.
- As a class, write a short summary of what happens in the extract. Then split pupils into groups and ask them to perform it. Encourage them to think about different ways of presenting the story, e.g. with a narrator reading the extract, by creating dialogue for the characters or with sound effects but no speech.
- *Beowulf* was written during the Anglo-Saxon period. Introduce pupils to some Anglo-Saxon history — where the Anglo-Saxons came from, when they came to England and what sort of lives they lived. Ask pupils to research the Anglo-Saxon burial site at Sutton Hoo in East Anglia. They should use their findings to write a newspaper report about the 1939 discovery of the ship buried there.
- Explain to pupils that this poem is set in Scandinavia, which is a region of Europe. Ask pupils if they know which countries are in Scandinavia and see if they can identify the region on a map. Then ask pupils to research one Scandinavian country and come up with a list of 'top ten' facts about it.

Cyber-Bullying

Cyber-Bullying

HALF of all young people say that cyber-bullying is part of everyday life

Question Book:
Year 6, pages 26-27

Author / Source:
www.dailymail.co.uk

Genre:
Non-fiction — newspaper article

Cross-curricular links:
- PSHE (safety online; bullying)
- Drama (performance)

Introduction

The Internet plays an increasingly important role in the social lives of young people, and almost all young people in Britain have regular access to a computer or a smartphone. This article looks at how children are more vulnerable to cyber-bullying as a result. Whilst protective measures like installing filters do help to protect young Internet users, many parents feel ill-equipped to deal with cyber-bullying and its effects. Before reading the article, ask pupils how many hours a day they spend on the Internet.

Answers

1. E.g. Because the newspaper wants to emphasise how shocking this statistic is.
2. E.g. He wants the Government to make sure cyber-bullying is taught in schools.
3. E.g. That cyber-bullying often involves someone writing a nasty comment in an email, text message or on social media. Because these comments are written down, they don't "disappear" like verbal abuse.
4. E.g. Yes, because bullies are less likely to be punished if nobody knows who they are.
5. E.g. Because the Internet is such a huge part of young people's lives that there's no way a victim could truly "unplug". Also, switching off devices doesn't solve the problem, it just ignores it.
6. Any appropriate answer. E.g. No, because people should be allowed to express themselves freely on the Internet and there will always be people who bully others. OR E.g. Yes, because people are becoming more aware of cyber-bullying and introducing new ways to stop it.

Extra Activities

- Tell pupils that a lot of non-fiction writing includes facts and statistics. Explain the difference between them, then, as a class, identify examples of each from the extract. Discuss why writers might include facts and statistics in their writing. (E.g. to make their arguments more persuasive, to back up their claims.)
- As a class, discuss different strategies pupils can use to deal with cyber-bullying and how to stay safe online (telling a parent or teacher, blocking bullies on social media, not giving out personal details etc.). Using their ideas, ask pupils to make a leaflet aimed at younger students to help them stay safe online.
- Show pupils a short clip about cyber-bullying, e.g. 'Cyber Bullying Virus' made by the charity Cybersmile. Ask pupils whether they liked it or not, and whether they thought it was effective. Divide pupils into small groups and ask them to create their own piece of drama designed to raise awareness about the dangers of cyber-bullying. The performance should be no more than 5 minutes long.
- As a class, create a mind map of the different types of bullying behaviour. Ensure children are aware that bullying isn't just physical violence or name calling, it can also be isolating someone or a friend controlling your actions. Then ask pupils to create their own mind maps about the effects that bullying can have on someone, e.g. becoming withdrawn, having fewer friends, acting aggressively, skipping school. Then, as a class, make a list of the positive actions pupils can take to support someone who is being bullied, e.g. making them feel included, standing up for them, telling a teacher if they see bullying behaviour.

Romeo and Juliet

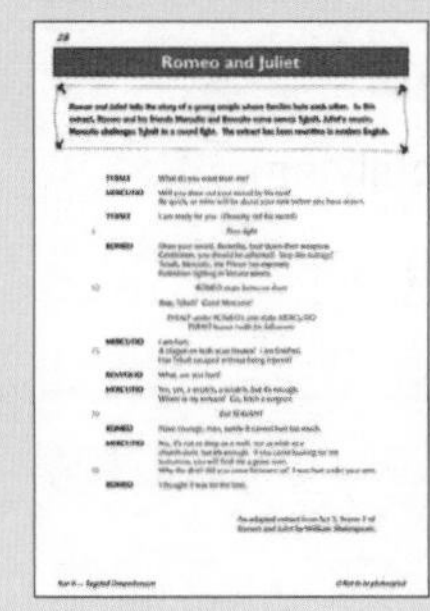

Question Book:
Year 6, pages 28-29

Author / Source:
William Shakespeare (adapted)

Genre:
Classic fiction — playscript

Cross-curricular links:
- Drama (performance)
- Art (wanted posters)
- History (Shakespeare)

Introduction

Romeo and Juliet is one of Shakespeare's most well-known tragedies. The play explores the themes of love, family and fate, as two young lovers from rival families try to overcome the feud that divides their households. Although this extract has been rewritten into modern English, it retains some of the imagery used by Shakespeare in the original playscript. Some pupils may find the extract difficult to follow at first, but reading the extract several times or focussing on one character at a time may help to consolidate understanding.

Answers

1. "Will you draw out your sword by his ears?"
2. E.g. Enthusiastic, because he starts the fight with Tybalt. He also warns him to "Be quick" or else he'll begin to attack before Tybalt is ready.
3. E.g. Romeo tries to break up the fight between Tybalt and Mercutio, but Tybalt stabs Mercutio under Romeo's arm and then leaves.
4. a. Romeo and Tybalt b. E.g. That both of their families should be punished for Mercutio getting stabbed.
5. E.g. Guilty, because his friend was hurt when Romeo tried to break up the fight.
6. Any appropriate answer. E.g. Yes. Mercutio thinks that he's going to die because he says that by tomorrow he will be "a grave man" and implies that the wound is "enough" to kill him. OR E.g. No, because I think Mercutio is overreacting. Romeo says "surely it cannot hurt too much".

Extra Activities

- As a class, rewrite this extract as part of a novel. Remind pupils that they'll need to add descriptions and consider how different characters might be feeling at different points in the extract.
- The story of Romeo and Juliet has been retold in many different formats. Give pupils a simple summary of the play, then show them an example of a modern written adaptation and its blurb, e.g. *Daz 4 Zoe* by Robert Swindells. Ask pupils to think of their own modern-day version and create a blurb for it.
- Shakespeare created and popularised many words that are still used in the English language today. Challenge pupils to research words that he invented and ask them to come up with amusing Shakespearean insults, e.g. 'You zany, frugal moonbeam!' Read the best ones out to the class.
- Split the class into groups of four. Ask each group to memorise the extract and perform it to the class. Pupils should then vote for their favourite performance, explaining the reasons for their choice.
- Explain that after this scene, Romeo kills Tybalt and flees. Ask pupils to design a wanted poster for Romeo. The poster should tell people what happened between Romeo and Tybalt and whether a reward is offered. It should also instruct the public on what to do if they see Romeo.
- As a class, make a list of the kinds of information usually included in a biography. Then ask pupils to use the list to research Shakespeare. Pupils should use their findings to create a short biography about him.

A Letter from a Former Slave

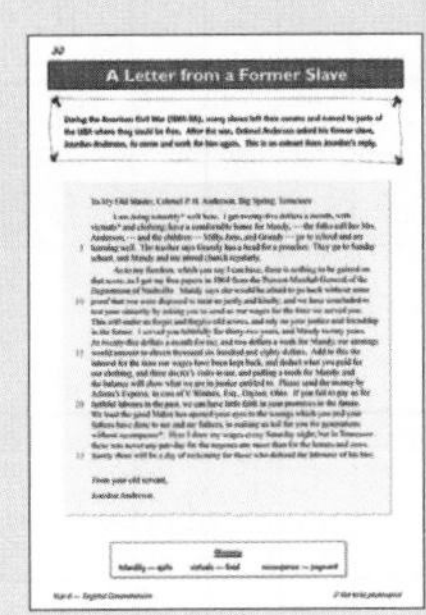

Question Book:
Year 6, pages 30-31

Author / Source:
Jourdon Anderson

Genre:
Non-fiction — letter

Cross-curricular links:

- History (slavery; abolitionism)
- PSHE (modern slavery; freedom)

Introduction

Between the 1500s and the early 1800s, Britain was heavily involved in the Atlantic slave trade. Britain abolished the slave trade in 1807 and outlawed slavery in most of the British Empire in 1833. In the USA, however, slavery remained central to the society and economy of many southern states. It was only at the end of the American Civil War in 1865, that slavery was abolished throughout the USA. This letter, written in August 1865, offers a fascinating insight into one freed slave's attitude towards his former master. Before pupils read the letter, make sure they understand the concept of slavery, and explain that in the USA slaves were forced to work in brutal conditions on sugar, cotton, tobacco and rice plantations.

Answers

1. E.g. To show that he doesn't need to go back to work for the Colonel because things are much better for him now than when he was a slave.
2. E.g. That he doesn't need the Colonel to give him his freedom because he's already officially free.
3. E.g. Because she's worried that he might treat them badly or force them to be slaves again.
4. a. E.g. To pay the money he owes Jourdon and Mandy for all the years they worked for him as unpaid slaves. b. Any appropriate answer. E.g. Yes, because it was unfair for the Colonel to benefit from Jourdon and Mandy's hard work when they didn't get anything in return.
5. E.g. People who don't pay their workers will be punished in the end.
6. Any appropriate answer. E.g. He feels angry about the way the Colonel treated him in the past — he says what the Colonel did was wrong and calls it fraud. He also feels that the Colonel isn't really trustworthy — he doesn't want to work for him because he doesn't think he will keep his promises.

Extra Activities

- Ask pupils to identify features of the text that show it is a letter. What other layout features are usually found in formal letters? Get them to create a labelled template explaining how to set out a formal letter.
- Get pupils to research the countries involved in the slave trade, and the movement of slaves and the goods they produced around the world. Ask them to produce a map labelling the countries involved and the different commodities that were traded, e.g. sugar, rum, tobacco, cotton and coffee. Are pupils shocked to learn that slavery played such a central role in the global economy?
- Explain to pupils about the abolition movement. Show them images designed by abolitionists to campaign against slavery, such as Josiah Wedgwood's 'Am I not a man and a brother?' Pupils should then produce their own poster to support the abolition movement.
- Explain to pupils that millions of adults and children are still treated as slaves today. Ask pupils to write a speech arguing for the abolition of modern slavery.
- Ask pupils to explain what freedom means to them. Are the pupils' ideas about freedom similar or different? Why is freedom important? How do they think it would feel to lose their freedom?

Pupil Progress Chart — Year 3

Average score out of 10																														
Sir Gawain and the Green Knight																														
Nepal Earthquake Appeal																														
Oliver Twist																														
Labels on Children's Food																														
Sky Island																														
Plastic Bag Tree																														
Chicken School																														
Echo Effects																														
Mr Gum and the Biscuit Billionaire																														
Caring for Dogs and Puppies																														
Poems about Teachers																														
The Reluctant Dragon																														
Pioneer Children																														
An Interview with Andy Seed																														
The Three Nanny Goats Gruff																														
Class .... Pupil Name																														

☐ = non-fiction ■ = fiction

Pupil Progress Chart — Year 4

Average score out of 10																														
The Jungle Book																														
A Letter from Barack Obama																														
The Lion, the Witch and the Wardrobe																														
Wayne Rooney: Captain of England																														
Poems about the Weather																														
Escape from Germany																														
An Interview with Tim Peake																														
Coram Boy																														
The Story of Nu Wa																														
Armoured Dinosaurs																														
Julius Caesar's Goat																														
GRRRR																														
The Dragonsitter's Island																														
Geocaching																														
The Diary of a Killer Cat																														
Class .... **Pupil Name**																														

☐ **= non-fiction** ☐ **= fiction**

Pupil Progress Chart — Year 5

Average score out of 10	
Steve Jobs' Biography	
The Highwayman	
Harambe the Gorilla	
The Hound of the Baskervilles	
Candara's Gift	
Robot on the Ice	
Cora and the King	
The Oak and the Linden Tree	
Poems about Words	
Facts about Hurricanes!	
Goodnight Mister Tom	
Johnny and the Dead	
Baby Birds	
The Unluckiest Boy in the World	
Gertrude Ederle	
Class .... **Pupil Name**	

☐ = non-fiction ▨ = fiction

ECT221